Social Work Practice

An Introduction

Second Edition

Veronica Coulshed

MACMILLAN

First edition 1988
Reprinted once
Second edition 1991

Published by
MACMILLAN PRESS LTD
Houndmills, Basingstoke, Hampshire RG21 6XS
and London
Companies and representatives
throughout the world

ISBN 0–333–55905–3
ISBN 0–333–55909–6

A catalogue record for this book is available
from the British Library.

13 12 11 10 9 8 7 6
03 02 01 00 99 98 97 96

Printed in Hong Kong

For my mother

Contents

Acknowledgements

I appreciate all the suggestions for the second edition which I received from practitioners, students, family and friends. Special thanks are due to my husband, who is always generous with his time.

VERONICA COULSHED

Introduction

I am grateful for the opportunity to do a second and new edition of this book: there are always items in the first version which could have been said differently and better. Then again, knowledge in social work changes so rapidly that one almost wants to rewrite as soon as the first account appears. It is a welcome chance to incorporate the feedback from readers and reviewers, so that certain issues and methods of practice have received more attention. References for further reading, essential in an introductory text, are broad and up to date, although you will find that I have hung on to 'favourite' and seminal material in order to deepen the knowledge which has to be distilled here.

The purpose of the book remains the same – to help students and practitioners in field and group care to apply theory to their practice. In selecting a range of methods of intervention, the focus has been on developing core skills which are useful across the range of settings and client groups and to show, through the use of practice examples, how theory informs and improves practice. I shall come back to this point about what is theory and how it relates to practice in a moment.

I want, in this new edition, to restate the message that there are no easy remedies in social work, especially when we are confronted daily with oppression and deprivation. The problem with putting together an eclectic range of approaches is that they may appear like menus for success. Readers may asume that if they follow the strategies and techniques that planned outcomes will be achieved. No

1

technique or theory can do this. Neither can we afford to overlook what England (1986) describes as the intuitive use of one's self, including the quality of the relationships which we work to build. These remain at the heart of what we do well. While it is true that people do not come to us looking for a relationship, and while it is no substitute for practical support, nevertheless we are one of the few groups who recognise the value of relating to others in a way which recognises their experience as fundamental to understanding and action. This is not to advocate an anti-theoretical or atheoretical stance: those who discount intellectual scrutiny and rigour undermine the credibility of our profession (rushing about merely doing might say more about needing to be helpful as opposed to trying to understand the meaning of someone else's experience). What we do need to rec- ognise and congratulate ourselves for is, unlike other profes- sions such as the law, we are ahead of the field in trying to bridge the theory–practice divide (Vernon *et al.*, 1990).

In the original book it was acknowledged that whatever methods of helping are used these are constrained by the agencies within which we operate. Perhaps we are only as competent and effective as our systems allow us to be? Unfortunately, there is insufficient space in one volume to fully address the contexts in which practice takes place but it is hoped that the case examples cited throughout the text can be viewed against the backcloths of the various settings from which the referrals arose. I have since written about man- agement in social work (Coulshed, 1990) and how this has an impact on work and workers, but it may require readers, when studying the case examples, to accept that in each instance the approach undertaken was inevitably enhanced or limited by the purpose, policy, procedures, material resources and staff available in each specific organisation.

It is important too to restate, especially when, as here, the focus is on working with individuals, families and groups, that frequently systems changing is more effective and preferable to people changing. Where large scale and rapid intervention is required, for example the programmes set up to cope with disasters in recent years, devising new struc- tures and organisational delivery mechanisms can be seen to be more urgent in the first instance than concentrating on 'micro' methods of intervention – though these become priority later. We are agents of our agencies to whose purposes and structures we look whenever large issues need tackling.

In fact, those numerous changes which have affected the very nature of social work and patterns of administration in recent years exemplifies this. New legislation, changing structures and different funding mechanisms are beginning to alter our purpose, roles and tasks. Community care initiatives, in particular, have demanded that we learn skills such as budgeting as well as giving prominence to indirect practice competencies such as resource building and mobilisation. Accordingly, this shift of emphasis is reflected in forthcoming chapters, representing social work as it really is, rather than as we might like it to be (Bar-On, 1990). At the same time, though happy to track these developments and anticipate others, I have deliberately not 'thrown the baby out with the bathwater'. Human beings remain at the centre of our concern, the *raison d'être* of our enterprises; thus, face-to-face work is a prominent part of this account of social work practice.

The original book was written because of a concern that our traditional approaches were being misshapen or lost. We were beginning to feel embarrassed with words such as 'casework', apologetic about looking for deeper meanings which people attach to events in their lives and inhibited about wanting to be creative and instinctive when occasion fitted this. Though critics would have us start afresh, innovators who have shaped alternative practices, for instance community social work (Hadley *et al.*, 1987), are beginning to recognise the need for interpersonal as well as entrepreneurial skills (although they still criticise what they amusingly term 'client-centred, esoteric methods').

Choosing among alternative approaches

Let us hope that the ideas contained in this volume are not seen as 'esoteric'; the approaches chosen for analysis are meant to stimulate practitioners to make a well-rounded assessment and to plan a purposeful intervention based on

4 Social Work Practice

this. In order that social workers go beyond being themselves, yet become more themselves, they possibly need to relax knowing that now and then there are patterns and regularities in the way that people and systems behave: knowing what is going on and having some starting points in the shape of practice theories may permit practitioners to become confident and therefore competent in what they undertake. I know that students and myself benefit from having problem solving methods to choose from rather than haphazardly reacting in an increasingly desperate fashion to what is presented. The essential point though, is, when choosing to follow a particular approach, this must be determined by the needs of the client/user of the service – we must never make the person fit the method.

So, how do we go about choosing among alternative approaches? Is there a 'right' method for each case? Learners frequently ask this but in our present state of knowledge we cannot claim that following a systematic 'treatment' plan will invariably produce expected results. Only in a limited way is this reliable. We know, for example, that letting someone talk to a counsellor who conveys empathy, a non-possessive warmth and genuineness is one way of facilitating self-initiated solutions; research by Truax and Carkhuff (1967) and the work of the late Carl Rogers (1980) actually states that these are core conditions for helping and change. At the other end of the spectrum, it is possible to predict the increased likelihood of a positive outcome using behavioural methods such as desensitisation in treating say someone with a phobic disorder. When large scale tragedies occur, disaster management teams move in prepared to adopt a crisis intervention approach, more or less certain that this will match the needs of the majority of the sufferers in the early post-trauma stages.

Essentially, there is a tendency to leave the choice of intervention very much up to the workers who must choose a pathway which:

– fits the goals decided upon by worker and/or clients
– matches the needs of the client, e.g. for environmental manipulation or building self-esteem etc.

- has been shown to have some effectiveness in the given circumstances
- fits the capacities of the client, the worker and the agency
- is feasible in terms of time and other resources available
- takes into account the influence of other systems in the network.

What is not advisable is:

- having no method at all and just 'doing' social work (as if this can somehow not involve having a view of how people 'tick' and what values are held)
- doing exactly the opposite and clinging to a preferred 'school' of thought (I have known students be entranced by family therapy, cognitive therapy, transactional analysis and the like, and be quite dogmatic about refusing to consider alternative tools)
- being whimsical about the choice of approach, dipping into a 'rag-bag' of ill-thought through ideas and techniques
- again conversely, not being willing to experiment a little (by testing out more systematically one's own interventive strategies which seem to work we thereby develop new, creative ideas from modest, even home-spun theories)
- finding that a chosen route is not effective, not changing to a more productive plan of action
- failing to evaluate efforts, whatever the chosen course
- declaring that, having tried the approach, it does not work; this is the same as saying, 'I tried piano playing once, I didn't think much of the tune'. All methods require practice and some skill.

The relevance of theory to practice

Let us go back now to what was said at the outset about how theory informs and improves practice. In years past students would not be readily convinced of this. They might protest that it was necessary to forget theory once in practice placements; that it reduced spontaneity and caring for people; theory implied distance and objectivity which contrasted with feelings and the loving reality of social work encounters; theory was seen as a stumbling-block towards developing one's individual style; the most that could be hoped for was students admitting that they might subconsciously be using theory which they had absorbed during training. Thankfully, current students are less antagonistic to theoretical ideas, naming and trying to integrate what can at first glance appear to be a smorgasbord of apparently contradictory explanations of behaviour.

To take the last point further a little: some educationalists have debated at length that there are competing positions regarding social reality and the production of knowledge (i.e. theory); (see, for instance, Rojek, 1986, 1986; Howe, 1987). Gradually, it is being acknowledged by such thinkers and others that a 'gladiatorial paradigm', that is the notion that social work theories compete and cannot be integrated since they offer opposing interpretations of social reality, ignores the commonalities and interdependence of explanations of how human beings shape and are shaped by their internal and external worlds.

Either/or arguments, such as insisting that counsellors must be either Rogerian or behaviourist, or that social workers are either radical or traditional in their approach, fail to see the underlying continuities which hold together such apparently diverse positions. Most theories have elements in common as well as elements in opposition: Howe (1987) shows how the so-called eclectic helper, who claims to take the best bits from different theories, actually holds a consistent view of people and their situations. Purists might attack this seemingly undisciplined and incoherent way of working; yet, I believe that this is the way in which practice is generally conducted at present. However, explorations into how the growing proliferation of methods and therapies might be integrated, at least into 'families' which share a common vocabulary plus a pool of concrete, specific operating procedures, is going ahead (see, for example, Mahrer, 1989).

Before we go any further, perhaps it would be useful to actually examine what the term 'theory' might mean. Often, at the outset of training, students become afraid of the expectation that they learn theory and apply it to practice.

Their confusion is understandable; unfortunately, teachers use the word to mean many different things.

One of the ways in which we talk about theory is when we are thinking about what are called Grand theories; Freudian or Marxist explanations of what is human nature fall into this category. Mid-range theories are not so comprehensive; they address particular phenomena such as loss, attachment, delinquency and so on and try to explain their causes and consequences. The problem when we talk about 'social work theory' is that we could, moreover, be referring to at least three different possibilities – do we mean theories *of* social work, what it is, who is it for etc.; are we using the phrase to mean how to do social work (essentially the practices in this book which identify theories *for* social work, implying that there is a theory of social work activity); or are we referring to those social science disciplines which offer us a range of explanations and contrasting views of human nature which ought to thereby shape our endeavours? Taking yet further examples; Pilalis (1986) unveils six meanings of 'theory' which reflect the visions which are carried amongst the student group. Some see it as a general rule or law which is testable against observable evidence; others, similarly influenced by the physical sciences perhaps take it to mean a probability, a hypothesis or a speculative explanation subject to research; when we move to the third and fourth meaning we in the human sciences are taking the word to mean a system of principles which help us to understand events more clearly or to capture, for practical purposes, underlying ideological and value bases of say psychological, sociological or political ideas. Popular uses of the word 'theory' are encapsulated in the fifth and sixth examples, that is the way in which students distinguish it from practice ('this is theory rather than practice') and the dismissive, 'that is all very well in theory' which sees knowledge as idealistic and goals unattainable.

It is no wonder that, unless we unravel all these different usages at the outset, a group of learners will remain resistant to the notion of a practice informed and enlarged by theory, whether this be the Grand and mid-range theories (analysed in the books by Howe, 1987 and Hardiker and Barker,

1981), or those written about here which map out models and methods of social work intervention. Of fundamental importance, as stated earlier, is that social work theory should never become an end in itself. It should serve the following functions: it should provide some explanation for the complexities we observe in our practice so that out of apparent chaos we might expose patterns and regularities in behaviour and situations; it should thereby help us to predict future behaviour, and how the problem or condition could develop and what might be the effect of planned change.

In addition, a truly useful theory would provide guidance towards a more effective practice, giving a measure of confidence so that we do not feel totally at the mercy of our working environment; if we build on and record effective strategies and techniques, we then build transmittable knowledge by directing others to what is common and regularly occurring in human experience. Theory fulfils a boundary setting function too, assisting the identification of those domains where the theory for practice is relevant or not; and, finally, having a body of accepted theories of practice helps novices to internalise basic professional knowledge and values by which they may explain to themselves and others what they are doing and why. To reiterate what was said in the first edition of this text; theoryless practice does not exist; we cannot avoid looking for explanations to guide our actions, while research has shown that those agencies which profess not to use theory offer a non-problem-solving, woolly and directionless service (Corby, 1982).

Furthermore, when we evaluate our efforts, be they services to individuals or whole programmes of care, we begin to engage in theory building. Much social work theory derives from someone's experience which they have written down and shared with others.

This is why I propose that our job is an intellectual one; it demands the rigour of the practitioner–researcher who can think and do, who can use heart and head, who can incorporate reading and research so as to liberate practice. The educationalist/community worker Freire (1972) calls this ability to think and do 'praxis'; he encouraged people to perceive, interpret, criticise and transform the world around them. In social work a lot of time is spent in giving tangible, immediate, practical help but this does not invalidate attempts to look beyond the obvious to ensure that people get the thoroughness of the service they need. Today's social service departments rely on staff who have more than the 'right' personality to do the work; they also have to demonstrate capacities for comprehensive data collection, assessment, a repertoire of interventive skills and a knowledge of evaluative mechanisms.

The processes of social work have become more complex in recent times so that if we have a variety of tools in our workbag we are more able to offer a service which is determined by client need rather than our own limitations. Although it could be argued that the ideal would be to match the client with what the worker can offer (so that someone, for instance with a concrete behavioural difficulty is helped by a behavioural worker), it is far better if each individual gets to grips with a range of approaches and methods mainly by keeping up with the literature and sharing expertise with colleagues. I hope that this book is one step towards this.

Chapter 1 discusses the core skills of case management and considers interviewing, assessing and recording; the new emphasis on multidisciplinary assessment is given attention and the scope of assessments widened to take into account the growing need to assess not only people but also organisational systems. Thus, information on how to assess an elderly person's home is dealt with in some detail. Then Chapter 2 looks specifically at ways of problem solving by using counselling methods and other case management practices such as networking and mobilising resources. These appear like a hotch-potch of interventions but they all rely on good interpersonal and organisational skills as we shall see. Social workers deal not only with people in crisis, but whole communities and systems in crisis (for instance the way that some agencies react towards someone who is the victim or perpetrator of sexual abuse); Chapter 3 offers some techniques and a theoretical framework for crisis intervention and disaster management in order to help individuals and whole communities to cope with catastrophes in their lives. A method of problem solving which can similarly lend itself to many levels and size of system is task-centred work, reviewed in Chapter 4. Practitioners are quite familiar with and therefore tend to use the approaches outlined in these first chapters; the later chapters focus on what might be viewed as specialist methods, though my intention is that they become part of everyone's armoury of knowledge and skill.

Two major schools of thought, the psychosocial and the behavioural approach, are explained in Chapters 5 and 6 respectively. Both have been misconceived and criticised. Psychosocial methods are the oldest in social casework, at one time seen by radicals as a form of policing the poor, forcing them to accept and adjust to the status quo. On occasion, clients' socio-economic positions were neglected, as was concerted action aimed at bringing about social change. However, as current analysts point out (Rojek *et. al*, 1988) opponents of individual methods themselves were prone to uncritical acceptance of 'received ideas'; Marxist slogans of exploitation and oppression were bandied about; such language, as they suggest, constructs reality (just as casework language does), rather than reflects it. Similarly, behaviour modification, and its use in institutions to make people conform was rightly condemned; in Chapter 6 I explore some current therapies whose ethics are less dubious.

Working with families and couples is explored in Chapter 7. Family systems therapy is outlined, together with everyday skills which can be used to help families with problems of getting along together. Chapter 8 introduces working with groups, analysing different models of groupwork and ways of handling difficult dynamics. As a concluding note I consider the need for good endings: literature in social work emphasises the need for good beginnings and 'engagement' but at times forgets to address the issue of terminating help (as I did in the first edition!).

Many of the chapters include frameworks which summarise the main ideas. I hope that these will be found useful in comparing one approach with another and in getting hold of the focal components of knowledge and skill. Throughout, I have referred to case examples. (Incidentally, use of the word 'case' is not meant to undervalue people or to harden what is a human-to-human encounter—it is used as short-hand for looking at the circumstances of a particular subject.) I trust that the use of real situations, with names changed to protect privacy, will help to bring theory 'alive'.

1

Case Management: Interviewing, Assessment and Recording

Interestingly, the title case manager is beginning to be applied to those who were once called caseworkers and latterly to social workers who take this up as a distinct profession. This trend may reflect the complexity of social service delivery systems, underlining the need for practitioners, whether or not they carry this title, to be able to organise and co-ordinate services across a range of field, day and residential settings, drawing on natural, voluntary, private and statutory sources of help. The case management process aims to achieve planned goals using what are familiar and central tasks in social work, namely data collection, analysis and planned intervention (what again long ago, modelled on medicine, were called study, diagnosis and treatment). In addition, case management, which is defined as a 'strategy for organising and coordinating care services at the level of the individual client' (Challis *et al.*, 1990, p. 5) depends on the same practice skills such as interviewing, communicating, assessing, recording, counselling and mobilising resources, which are covered in this and subsequent chapters. However, to direct our attention to the neglected arena of long-term, ongoing work, and to provide fresh impetus to the need for thorough assessments, case management has been developed into a circular process of case finding and screening → assessment → planning → monitoring and review → (and eventual closure).

Before we proceed, though, the nature of case management may still be unclear and the mystique which has surrounded its re-emergence in the recent past could add to misunderstandings. As can be seen above, case management has always been with us inasmuch as it relates to social work as a problem-solving process which relies on a mixture of administrative efficiency alongside what the North Americans call 'clinical' skills, i.e. social work practice and human relationship skills. A helpful article which aims to sort out the confusion is that by O'Connor (1988) where he tries to show the distinction between case management as a *system* and as a *practice*. In some ways, community care packages are examples of the former, where agencies have devised policies and programmes, job designs, staff training, arrangements with other organisations and so on in order to implement the performance of case management as a practice. In some respects everyone from the director down practises case management, but the levels of responsibility, autonomy, authority, complexity and direct practice differ depending on one's job function and the target/focus for one's efforts. Stress on various tasks and skills differs too so that programme development might be the main feature of a team leader's job while personnel such as social workers might rely more on direct skills such as those written about here. For readers wishing to pursue the notions of case management a major contribution is that by Challis and Davies (1989).

So to the core skills of case management: interviewing and communicating, highlighting initial contacts and barriers to communication, are examined first, noting too the importance of sensitive questioning which avoids an interrogative style. Next, the nature of assessment is explored using examples of an individual assessment, an assessment of a residential home and that of multidisciplinary assessments. To end the chapter various forms of record keeping are outlined.

Interviewing and communicating

Prior to making contact with a social service agency, the majority of people have usually considered other options such as seeking advice from friends and relatives. Clients may have picked up the phone numerous times and entry into the system is, to them, a giant step. It never ceases to amaze me that the public perceive us as powerful, authoritarian figures and so we need to be aware of fear as a theme in the pre-contact phase and develop ways of reaching out especially with oppressed groups and those who are unwillingly referred to us. Early interviews are often concerned with screening to see if the person is eligible for service and then if this is the case the potential client becomes an actual client or service user. Much, then, depends on the quality of interviewing. Amongst the large number of books on the subject, a favoured one by students and practice teachers is that by Garrett (1972). Despite first being published in 1942 it remains relevant today mainly because, as the Foreword says, it is a classic work, translated into many languages and timeless in its relevance to many settings. It is therefore recommended as initial reading. No matter how much we engage in interviewing (in residential centres and group care this might be more accurately described as communicating or interacting), it should never become routine. It is both art and science, a real encounter which relies on the worker's self-knowledge as well as uncommon knowledge about what makes people 'tick'. Beginners to interviewing require a knowledge of both manifest and less obvious reasons why human beings behave in the ways that they do, in other words what motivates people. Such knowledge promotes tolerance and effectiveness. Thus, a student recently was able to see that, while asking for an outside handrail for her elderly mother, the daughter who made the request needed to have this turned down so as to dissuade her frail parent from attempting to leave the house unaided. What was a seemingly simple situation in the routine task of a duty interview turned out to need a grasp of underlying psychological drives and feelings.

Only by carefully listening and observing the way that people seek help can objective facts and subjective feelings be part of an interpersonal exchange which correctly receives overt and covert messages, decodes them and responds to the various levels of communication therein.

People can say one thing but their behaviour says the opposite. Advanced practitioners, such as those who are expert in family therapy, moreover, are able to use the literal message, alongside what is known as the 'metamessage' (which are messages about the message), as part of their interviewing. An illustration of this might be the crucial stage of leaving home for adolescents; here mixed messages are frequently sent by them to their parents which the bracketed phrase, 'Can I [let you let me] leave?' reveals. Even if beginners cannot use this level of communication in interviews it is worthwhile at least being able to spot these kinds of underlying motivation.

Basic skills also involve the ten principles listed by Davies (1985) namely: letting the interviewee know how much time there is; starting where the client is in their understanding of the situation; trying to be sympathetic so as to help make the atmosphere a relaxed one; trying to see things through the other person's eyes; knowing the danger of passing judgement rather than acceptance; developing social skills such as smiling to help open up communication at the outset; avoiding questions that can be answered 'yes' or 'no'; not putting answers in the client's mouth; not probing too deeply too quickly and learning to cope with silences (which are usually the interviewee's best thinking times).

Each interview tends to have a focus, such as an exploration of someone's financial needs, illnesses, offences, relationships or whatever; at the same time every interview ought to have a structure (i.e. a beginning, middle and end). Each interview needs to be reflected upon, reviewing aspects of the content later, if possible via a detailed record or (in certain agencies such as those using family therapies), by means of a video recording. But what to look for in the mass of material produced?

The first few words that the client speaks are often quite significant, for example, 'My wife though that you could help me . . .'; equally the last things said could reveal what attitude the person leaves with, for instance, 'I think I can cope now I've got the information'. Also, in a series of interviews, references to difficulties may be returned to or repetition even of denial that something is worrying may give clues to helping. Inconsistencies and gaps may be spotted, for instance mentioning one parent but never the other, or concealed meanings such as the sexually abused client who fears interference (being interfered with?). Also sudden changes in conversation topics may either reveal too hurtful material or the person may have associated one idea with another, so these too are worth noting.

As indicated, social work interviews have special characteristics which distinguish them from everyday conversations. They have a context or setting, are directed towards a particular purpose, work is usually of a planned duration or sometimes contracted and the development of relationship, positive or negative, is an inevitable part of the process. Let us consider the last point a little more. The first meeting between a potential service user and a worker, besides serving the function of information gathering which will be used jointly in decision making about the nature of the difficulties and how to intervene, has at least three further aims: it tries to secure a 'treatment alliance' whereby the worker conveys a wish to understand the other's thoughts and feelings; it tries to include a sense of hopefulness about being able to tackle the circumstances and it demonstrates to the applicant some of the ways in which the worker and the service works. Unless these factors are taken into consideration subsequent management of the situation could prove sterile; this is especially so when there is an apparently negative response to the interviewer.

Sometimes students are worried when they encounter people who are uncooperative and who, despite saying that they want help, seem to do all that they can to block it. Often the reason for this is that approaching a stranger for help could be an occasion for shame, high expectations, a sense of failure and an admission of dependency. The worker does not have to reveal intimate, embarrassing or frightening facts about her or himself and so there is understandable reluctance and anger on the part of the interviewee, which may, indeed, remind them of times past when similar interpersonal contacts proved unhelpful.

On occasion, practitioners equally get frustrated or anxious when service users do not return after one interview, feeling that somehow they have failed. In fact, research shows that up to 50 per cent of help-seekers do not return for a second interview and while the quality of the initial session is related to a positive response, other reasons for non-continuation are possible (Marziali, 1988). Many people are quite satisfied with the first session and decide that they do not require further assistance; others are not ready to commit themselves to ongoing intervention; a high proportion of people prefer to ask for help on an as-needed basis rather than have a regular series of meetings and others are so overwhelmed by the intensity or chronicity of their problems that they cannot use the help which is offered. But there are ways of conducting an initial intake interview (or phone call) which are more likely to establish a favourable climate for a therapeutic alliance, such as ensuring that there is congruence, i.e. agreement between worker and client about expectations of what can be done and being open and honest about what cannot be done. From the outset all parties should be aware of why they are meeting. Successful interviews do not depend on content (what was said) or if the client got what was asked for: a significant outcome for the first interview is for the worker to be perceived as someone who is able to understand what the client's concerns are and how they feel about their difficulties and how the worker in turn accepts and uses subjective feelings in the working relationship.

A positive outcome in interviewing relies also on trying to eliminate some of the barriers to communication which can result in misunderstandings. Apart from clients who have evident comprehension, hearing or speech disorders (which may require study into alternative methods of communicating), errors which even experienced interviwers make include anticipating what the other person is going to say or assuming that you have understood the meaning of the words and non-verbal cues. It is better to let the client talk freely at first if possible; this can counteract any tendency to be sure in advance what the other is saying or is about to say. (As a student I had an awful habit of ending other people's sentences!)

When individuals are allowed to tell their story in their own way it is surprising how often they come up with their own solutions. Stereotyping clients creates defences too, so that pigeonholing someone as black, middle class, confused, inadequate or whatever encourages premature judgements and hasty conclusions; people are too complex, subtle and dynamic to sum up rapidly. Using jargon also is an obvious obstacle to good interviewing; it distances worker and client so that with learners I acknowledge one language for the classroom and another one for practice – although always using unpretentious and simple communication is stressed as the ideal if one can acquire this. Using the client's own words and phrases is often useful; it says that you are listening attentively and at the same time conveys acceptance and respect for their way of putting things.

Naturally, inattentiveness is a major block to communication. Listening is of central importance, but more will be said about this when we examine counselling processes in the next chapter. What Garrett (1972) states as the fine art of *questioning* can be a tricky part of interviewing, therefore, let us take some time over this.

Asking 'good' questions

The purpose of interviewing is more often than not to gather information. One way of doing this, besides observation and listening, is to ask questions which get at the facts and feelings. The topic of questioning as an interpersonal skill has been dealt with comprehensively by authors who have compared the different techniques associated with questions asked in classrooms, courtrooms and by researchers, clinicians and social workers (see Dillon, 1990). For our uses though we need to emphasise the ways in which the method can either hinder or aid the helping process. Hence, an interviewer who poses questions accusingly or in a suspicious tone rather than in an interested and friendly way will arouse fear and antagonism. The wording of a question in this respect is less material than the manner and tone in which it is put. You might try asking the question, 'Are you looking for work?' using a range of inflections to illustrate this.

Again, asking too many questions could sound nosey or interrogative or asking too few may leave relevant features hidden. The pace at which questions are put needs to be at the client's pace otherwise more might be revealed than the person intended resulting in annoyance or reluctance to return to the agency again. On the other hand, it is very common amongst inexperienced people to avoid asking probing questions when clients hint at what they are worried about deep-down. Failing to pursue some areas in an interview might be related to needing to protect *ourselves* from pain or fear of unearthing material which is threatening or distressing; over-cautiousness or reticence can be a hindrance. Accordingly, if someone hints that they are so depressed that they wonder if life is worth living and then quickly move on to another subject, it might be worthwhile coming back to that idea again later, saying something like, 'Can you tell me more about that?' or 'I'm not sure if I understood earlier when you said . . .' which allows for elaboration if the person wants this; it also lets the worker check out perceptions and it conveys to the client that the worker can cope with the 'unacceptable' thoughts and feelings.

Another barrier can be created by overuse of the question 'Why?'. It seems to imply that someone should explain their behaviour and accordingly defences go up. In any event, people often do not know 'Why?' and may be seeking help to understand themselves and their situation more clearly. A 'What?' alternative is preferable and may reveal information useful to all involved in the interchange as happened when a worker, instead of asking an elderly person why she was afraid to go out, asked what she thought might happen if she did.

Skilful use of questions is sometimes overlooked in social work, as if it is something anyone can do. As opposed to collecting information which appears to only have value to the organisation (which increases resistance, e.g. in involuntary clients in probation), questioning is one way of actually starting off the processes of change. It is worth studying the range of good questioning techniques which can help others identify their experience, raise consciousness, solve problems and so on. A number of these are written about in the literature: Henderson and Thomas (1980) describe how community workers will deliberately ask naïve questions to prompt local residents to begin to question what they assume they cannot influence. Reporter type questions can sometimes achieve the same goal, as can the devil's advocate approach. Here the respondent is intentionally confronted with the arguments of opponents in order to trigger a change. Other ways of employing questions which hold the germs of possible change involve taking a one-down stance by saying, 'I could be wrong but . . .' 'I wonder . . .' or, 'I don't quite understand . . .' all of which stimulate people to step outside of their usual frame of reference to consider new possibilities, without the worker dragging out information. Similarly preaching or giving premature advice is prevented by a tentative helper rather than one who has all the ready answers. Another general guideline is to log awkward moments and return to them later when the client can cope with a specific question, perhaps acknowledging the awkwardness and underlining an earlier question by asking it again. Cognitive therapists, whose ideas stem from behaviour therapy, have expertise in asking questions which challenge negative thoughts or false assumptions to which those who are depressed are prone (see Scott, 1989); thus a patient who says that he has no friends will be queried about this, 'When you say that you have no friends do you mean that or do you mean that you have only one or two?' and, 'Is it true to say that you are *always* depressed, your diary indicates a slight lifting of mood in the mornings?'; so questions need to slow people down to check out the way that they automatically construe their world. These are somewhat specialised techniques and we will come to them in more depth in Chapter 6.

A further style of asking good questions is that known as 'circular questioning'. Developed within the family therapy field it assesses family functioning and interaction by asking one member of the family to comment on the relationship or behaviour of two other members. Thus, 'When your mother tries to get Andrew to go to school, what does your grandmother do?' and, 'Who do you think is closer to your father, your sister or your brother?' and so on. Circular questioning highlights different viewpoints giving feedback to everyone present while introducing new information about how each third party views relations between other dyads (Penn, 1982). (In essence, it sets behaviour within context.)

Hypothetical questions, starting with, 'What if?' are additionally revealing for all as are those which ask someone to describe their ideal solution (giving clues to people's goals and the way in which work might move forward). With one family whose twelve-year-old boy was referred by the GP because of 'dizzy spells' for which no physical cause had been found, I discovered that his baby sister had recently died and nobody had yet cried, including his mother and grandmother. I asked him, 'What if you cried, who would get most upset when you get upset, your mum or your grandma?' bringing out themes for all to consider.

Problem-posing questions are preferable to those ready answers which invade the competence of others. People often have their own ideas which can be 'unlocked': for example, a despairing group of unemployed people who said, 'We can't change their policies' were induced to rethink their powerlessness by a group leader who asked, 'Who are *they*, and what do we know of their policies?' In sum, asking good questions saves time, helps to engage rather than alienate clients and can be a tool for actually beginning to change a situation.

When interviewing children and adolescents I think the specialist literature should be consulted and practice gained through experience, courses and maybe micro skills teaching via video and live supervision. It seems that interviewers who are skilled in adult work can find it hard to communicate with children; of course we are still talking about one human being relating to another but, myself included, there is a tendency to concentrate too much on the formal elements of the interviewing task. For instance, using questions is different with children with whom, in fact-finding, one may need to be quite specific and direct. It is difficult not to offer suggestions as Piaget once admitted. Letting the child talk freely while gaining facts takes expertise. Gaining cooperation, timing, overcoming confusion, managing hostility, being spontaneous, getting the right surroundings, communicating through 'third things' (toys and analogies), awareness of cultural appropriateness etc. are perhaps more crucial than they already are when interviewing grown-ups. For further reading I like the books by Rich (1968) and Redgrave (1987).

In the same way I consider that interviewing through an interpreter is something of a specialised and advanced skill. Though outside the scope of an introductory text, below is a summary of the advice given in an article by Freed (1988). She sees the interpreter as a conduit, linking interviewer and interviewee and thus careful preparation of the interpreter for this role is necessary, emphasising confidentiality, neutrality, conveying the emotional tone of the interview and transmitting accurately what is being communicated. The social worker (whose experience may resemble watching a foreign film without subtitles), must pay attention to the seating arrangement, discuss with the client the interpreter's presence, provide assurances of confidentiality, be patient as the pace may be slow, respect the attitudes about social work in the person's country of origin, avoid working through children or relatives if this is indicated and review the content and process later to ensure that a proper level of understanding was reached. Naturally, agencies should offer services to non-English-speaking clients and train interpreters in functioning within that role. Even though Freed's paper concerned the unique skills of interviewing those who do not speak English, much of what she writes could well refer to communicating through an interpreter for deaf or deaf-blind service users.

Finally, to end this section on interviewing and communicating, when novices first try to engage in these processes they frequently ask for some basic tools by which to approach the task so that they do not feel totally out of control of what is going on. While I abhor the use of techniques in social work as gimmicks or what Whan (1983)

calls 'tricks of the trade', nevertheless perhaps the following
formula is a helpful standby. In fact-finding interviews it
might remind the interviewer to cover relevant ground by
remembering the 5WH test. This stands for sentences that
start with why (sparingly), who, what, when, where and
how? A blend of enquiries which address these areas will
reveal a lot of fundamental infomation. Thus, to give an
example, what is the problem, when did it start, who could
help, where should we aim to sort things out, how has the
person tried to cope, how do they think the worker can
help? In addition a text which has proved valuable for those
investigating the protection of children, in order to plan for
their long-term care, which contains common sense but vital
areas for exploration and ways of unearthing sound assessments through appropriate questions is that by the Social
Services Inspectorate (SSI), (Department of Health, 1988).
This brings us now to the topic of assessments, what they are
and how they are undertaken.

Assessment

One key feature of case management practice is assessment.
Assessment is an ongoing process, in which the client
participates, whose purpose is to understand people in
relation to their environment; it is a basis for planning what
needs to be done to maintain, improve or bring about
change in the person, the environment or both. The skill of
undertaking and producing an assessment depends on administrative talent coupled with human relations skills. It
takes someone who can organise, systematise and rationalise
the knowledge gathered together with a gift for sensitivity in
taking in the uniqueness of each person's situation. 'Hard'
knowledge such as facts are pertinent, but so too are
thoughts and feelings and the worker's own clarified intuition. Thus, while appreciating that documentation issued by
bodies like the Department of Health and the Social Services Inspectorate (referred to above) and their very useful
guidelines on assessment are essential everyday handbooks,

inexperienced workers need to learn the art as well as the science of carrying out this task: for example, noting how a family interacts with you as well as what they say. In fact, the SSI recognise process information as vital (Department of Health, 1988) and are themselves cautious about laying down universal prescriptions on how to do assessments and what to cover in them.

Sometimes beginners confuse the term assessment with evaluation and while there may be an evaluative component, e.g. measuring if a client, or a whole care programme, is accomplishing goals, assessments are more akin to an exploratory study which forms the basis for decision making and action. Similarly, assessment is not just an event, e.g. the production of a profile on someone or a report for the court; it is, as indicated, a way of continuously collecting and synthesising available data, which includes thoughts and feelings, in order to formulate 'treatment' plans. Assessment is therefore a process and a product of our understanding. It is on this basis of understanding people and circumstances that we reach initial appraisals or what used to be called 'diagnostic formulations' which:

- describe
- explain
- predict
- evaluate
- prescribe.

Traditionally, social work assessments, after certifying eligibility for services (case finding and screening), tended to follow what might be termed 'resource-led' pathways rather than a broader 'needs-led' approach (see Forder, (1974) for a discussion on what is meant by the concept of need). Good practice stems from open-minded and comprehensive assessments, avoiding the narrow focus of service-oriented assessments (Challis *et al.,* 1990). In other words, if we develop frameworks which separate out ends and means (what needs and goals could be met whether or not there are resources to achieve these), this larger picture will reveal service gaps adding possibilities for imaginatively filling these. Certainly in relation to elderly, frail people, these kinds of needs assessments have enabled creative services to happen: clients can be kept in the community longer with a better quality of life for themselves and their carers. An illustration of this occurred when a group of older people who tended to neglect their food, either because they had no appetite to eat alone, forgot to eat or were too physically frail to cook, were brought together in a local domiciliary helper's home for their meals, a service that was specifically designed to match their patterns of living.

In the same way, the components of a comprehensive assessment for children requires vision. A plan for long-term care would go beyond simply checking out the child's developmental history, significant people's perceptions about levels of care provided and the child's reactions. The child's own views, whether expressed verbally or non-verbally, and those of relevant participants to the assessment would be sought to get ideas about the best way of helping the child, regardless of whether such a service existed or could be afforded.

In reality, of course, needs-led principles cannot work unless there are plenty of resources; in social work we will always be in a position where demand exceeds supply, which is why so many agencies have introduced priority (i.e. rationing) systems. Nevertheless, if we do not move into the new era of community care with a widened vision we might continue to make our assessments fit into existing provision. Recently when talking to a case manager about the danger of doing assessments which heighten expectations, she reported that in ten years this had never happened: by closely involving individual users and any carers in assessment, it had actually had a therapeutic dimension, flexibly exploring with people what they wanted and working out together what could be created. Thus, assessment is seen as a part of the total service provision, not an isolated activity which serves organisational needs alone.

A literature search of what to explore in assessments (the content) will reveal that, depending on the circumstances of the referral, one could end up collecting vast amounts of material encompassing social, psychological, physical, economic, political and spiritual elements which compose an individual, a group, a family, a neighbourhood or an organisation. The source of the referral; details of the referrer, the client and the situation; the problem and its meaning for significant people; historical facts which impinge on the present; facts about age, ethnic origin, roles and behaviour, environment and informal networks; resources and strengths; other agencies involved and so on usually feature. (See suggestions such as those for *Assessment and Case Management* by the King's Fund Institute, 1990.)

I think that the skill in doing and recording an assessment lies in the ability to collect enough of the right kind of information. Frequently learners attempt to find out everything in a 'scatter-gun' method: they hope to find out something worthwhile by asking more and more questions resulting in confusion from an information overload. It is as well to remember that we will never know all there is to know about people or systems – assessments are always continuous and dynamic and, in this sense, never complete. In some ways too they are never 'true' inasmuch as they tend to be filtered through the assessor's perspective, despite attempts at exactness and comprehensiveness. An exercise I did with students revealed that 'What you see depends on where you look'; I split the group into three and gave each the same referral, merely emphasising that one group represented education social workers, another hospital social workers and the others were to pretend to be community workers. Each group produced a totally different set of questions by which to assess a teenager truanting from school, whose mother was depressed, whose father was unemployed, the family living in a deprived neighbourhood where government cutbacks had resulted in fewer services.

Another drawback to assessments, particularly when they are carried out by statutory agencies such as the probation service and personal social services departments, is that they could be used to control not just access to services but also to control disadvantaged sections of the community. Stigmatising and scapegoating of clients via negative assessments (see Jones, 1983) unfortunately does occur and, in fact, research shows that name-calling increases the longer a person is socialised into our profession. You may find that dossiers are kept on so-called 'problem families' or those who have assertively sought assistance. The adjective 'aggressive' is applied to black clients who assert their needs for equitable services, yet, as Ahmad (1990) shows, white assessment fails to take into account black realities and environments. Thorough assessments actually take a long time, often longer than can be coped with in most busy offices; so some of the problems to do with this function may also to related to worker stress as well as ignorance. I know that I became 'case-hardened' and cynical after a number of years practising in an overworked team and this no doubt affected the quality of assessments and my professional judgement. (I now try to treat every day as my first.)

Accuracy of factual content is essential. Systematic methods help, as we have seen, as does what might be called 'triangulation', where information is cross-checked with other sources. It is imperative that we do not rely on hearsay or gossip when assessments serve the purpose of planning and intervening in someone's life. Currently, it seems that assessments emphasise the worker's and the agency's needs: an alternative to this one-way approach is to share assessments with clients as the case manager above did. When this happens, not only is accuracy improved, but the basis for an honest exchange is laid down. Shared assessments engage the other and begin the process of change, giving priority to each participant's views. However, no matter how high our standards or the Utopian ideals of our critics, mistakes will be made. One of the commonest, I find, stems from prejudicial, one-dimensional views of situations: for instance; when working with families, workers see one point of view, identifying perhaps with an adolescent's complaint of strict parenting, or siding with one parent against another. The importance of professional supervision cannot be underestimated in assisting people to see beyond the obvious.

This brings us to the idea of sharing assessments with other colleagues as a way of reducing the risk of bias or error. (Multidisciplinary assessment will be dealt with later.)

There could be value in *team assessments*, as opposed to our usual practice of leaving this to one worker. Furthermore, in circumstances as important as, say, the delicate business of child placement (see Thoburn, 1988), the amount of information required about relationships, needs, sort of placement and so on demands that this be a shared study. Everyone who knows anything about the child can contribute. One social worker, faced with an eleven-year-old boy who had been in care most of his life, first of all read his file carefully. From this she constructed a flow chart diagram showing his numerous moves from one caretaker to another, noting that there were gaps in his history (which can happen if records are not meticulously kept). Within this factual flow chart she constructed an emotional one illustrating the feelings that the child experienced and those he had engendered in others, for example, 'distressed when moved into a large family'. Alongside this assessment instrument the family placement worker used others such as a family tree, an ecomap of her own team colleagues, a planning algorithm and a framework in which to analyse larger factors such as the legal context, agency considerations and public opinion. In collaboration with a student on placement and the key worker in the children's home, the worker set out to interview as many people as she could in the boy's past in order to piece together the jig-saw puzzle of his life. In this way too, the child's capacity for attachments could be assessed for the future.

Incidentally, work with this little boy, as well as the formal tools mentioned (see Bryer, 1989 for further examples), used games, exercises and playing to supplement the knowledge gained. These assessment methods also let the child gradually, over the course of eighteen months, open the door to his past, helped him cope with his losses, reliving his grief so that he could resolve it to make way for new attachments.

If we are to ensure that an optimum assessment can be done, given the detail implied in what this section has said up to now, then, as indicated, we need time. A practice teacher had completed four Social Enquiry Reports in one morning on a recent visit I made to a probation department. Given that such a report for the court about an alleged offence has to take into account due process, justice and welfare and has to clarify the balance between need, risk and resources for intervention, then it behoves organisations not to treat such assessments on an assembly line basis. In other settings, even bureaucratic ones which use proforma models for assessment, it has been possible to share the task with clients. Self-assessments are often seen as an enjoyable and informative source to youngsters in intermediate treatment programmes who learn from giving pen pictures of themselves, filling in easy questionnaires or paper tests and rating charts. Prospective foster families too are happy to be left to fill in self-assessment application forms by which they can describe themselves.

Computer-aided assessments may become time-savers. In medicine this technology can assist in formulating diagnoses and maybe social diagnoses will figure in our sphere eventually. Risk factors in child abuse have been produced for computer analysis; some time ago in Canada I used a program called FAM (Family Assessment Measure) by which individual members, prior to a family therapy session, answered computer-posed questions around themes of task accomplishment, roles, control, communication, affection, norms and values; and one of my students presently is feeding assessments on a community profile into a computer, noting the correspondence between rising crime rates and those for unemployment.

To recapitulate before we consider multidisciplinary assessments: an assessment is a perceptual/analytic process of selecting, categorising, organising and synthesising data. It is an exploratory study which avoids labels and is reached as a result of systematic and careful deliberation of needs, not simply what services are available. As well as facts it spans feelings, intuition, judgement, metaphors and meanings. Priority is given to the person's perceptions of their circumstances. Hasty prejudices are seen as undermining to particularly oppressed groups. Tools which are used may include questions, self-perception ratings, role play, problem checklists, pen pictures, diaries and other instruments found valuable by the consumer or the working team.

All assessments contain the risks of error or bias which might be partly counteracted by cross-checking data; extra suggestions for reducing worker bias include:

1. Improving self-awareness so as to monitor when you are trying to normalise, be over-optimistic or rationalise data.
2. Getting supervision which helps to release blocked feelings or confront denial of facts or coping with the occasional situation where you have been manipulated.
3. Being wary of standing in awe of those who hold higher status or power and challenging their views when necessary.
4. Treating all assessments as working hypotheses which ought to be substantiated with emerging knowledge; remember that they are inherently speculations derived from material and subjective sources.

Multidisciplinary assessments

Central to the community care proposals was the aim of creating individualised, flexible packages of care, workers arranging and providing services from independent, voluntary and statutory groupings: a key responsibility was collaboration with medical, nursing and other caring agencies (DoH, 1989).

With these systems in mind the case manager is the person who facilitates and co-ordinates a multidisciplinary assessment. In the case of health assessments of older people, these can take place at home, in a day or residential centre or in a hospital setting, and, to give a flavour of some of the dynamics of various professionals (for instance, health visitors, occupational therapists, physiotherapists, general practitioners, district nurses and social workers) working together, below is a summary of research findings into shared assessment of people who are elderly.

The study (Runciman, 1989) described what the different professional groups perceived as important to check in an assessment and devised a useful 'prompt list' of the content of the areas to explore. Briefly, these were:

– Mobility (inside/outside/steps/balance/joints etc.)
– Exercise (on exertion, e.g. chest pain, leg pain)

- Lower limbs (feet, circulation, ankles, ulcers)
- Skin (itching, pressure areas)
- Vision (reading, glasses)
- Hearing (door-bell, conversation, aids)
- Self-care (washing, bathing, toileting, dressing)
- Continence (bladder, bowels, day, night, frequency)
- House and household tasks (garden, heating, hazards, security)
- Nutrition (diet, appetite, cooking, weight, teeth/ dentures)
- Finance (benefits, pensions)
- Medication (drugs prescribed/taken, side-effects)
- Medical History
- Services (voluntary/private, HV, GP, home help, hospital)
- Mental status (memory, orientation, mood, sleep, grief)
- Attitudes (to health, housing, help, carers)
- Social support (relatives, friends, neighbours, amount, stress)
- Aids (walking, toileting, bathroom, kitchen)
- Communication (telephone, emergency help)

Professionals might agree about these categories, but the research revealed differences in perspectives – difficulties in rising from a chair, for example, might be assessed by a GP as arthritic hips, by a health visitor as a low chair or by a physiotherapist as poor hand function. Similarly, interesting differences in starting points or foci for assessment were noted, the social workers zoning in on attitudes, feelings and housing; occupational therapists, not surprisingly, starting with mobility. The groups differed as to whether or not they carried a framework for assessment in their head; where a particular theoretical framework had been adopted, e.g. amongst district nurses, this proved to be a barrier to more detailed considerations of need.

From this it is apparent that *multidisciplinary teamwork* is crucial whenever we attempt to pull together a rounded picture of someone's circumstances. Multidisciplinary teams consist of a number of different disciplines, whether or not in the same building, sharing their knowledge and expertise about a specific client with the objective of identifying and using those services which most effectively meet assessed needs (see Department of Health, 1989). If we concentrate on the role of the social worker in such a team, the kinds of skill called for include:

- *Partnership*, the ability to engage with colleagues, allocate tasks and give feedback.
- *Negotiation*, making clear what outcomes for self and others are desired; compromise and confrontation.
- *Networking*, gathering and disseminating information, linking people and establishing mutual support groups.
- *Communicating*, writing effective reports, speaking and writing in a non-jargonised way.
- *Reframing*, offering different perspectives by placing the problem in a wider frame of reference and discussing alternative ways of seeing the problem.
- *Confronting*, assertively challenging a dominant view.
- *Flexibility*, learning from the skills of others.
- *Monitoring and evaluation*, measuring outcome and modifying methods or goals accordingly (CCETSW/IAMHW, 1989).

Just as important, perhaps, is for the worker to be aware of funding complexities and blurring of team members' roles and tasks.

In addition, a sensible publication on multidisciplinary teamwork, produced by people who had worked in or received the services of multidisciplinary mental health teams (CCETSW/IAMHW, 1989) says that legal, social science theory, organisational and resource knowledge are a must for the social worker who wishes to be equipped for this kind of work: respect, openness and client-centredness too are requisite values if the worker is to make a distinctive contribution to the team. Otherwise, as they warn, the social worker could become either a hostile or marginal figure or, chameleon-like, opt to fit in with the view of the rest. They point out that consensus is not the goal of interdisciplinary working – conflict is central to success so that honest dialogue can expand everyone's skills and horizons.

I suppose that many of the tensions that arise amongst interdisciplinary team members relate to the myths and stereotypes that we hold about other professions. A joint seminar for doctors, health visitors and social workers resulted in a group of my students gaining more informed views about the training, goals, methods, values and power of the other professions and to increased confidence about forming good relationships (not least because the GPs were dressed casually, while the students wore smart clothes!). More seriously, stereotyping can be overcome via joint training, working and peer supervision activities in multi-disciplinary teams.

Assessing organisations

Part of the social work task revolves around our ability to assess and understand organisations, not only our own but those with which we interact. As stated earlier, effective case management concerns the matching of choices with resources. Let us take as a case study those older people who decide to live in residential homes as a positive solution to loneliness, increasing frailty or a desire for fulfilment through the use of recreational facilities. So, if such a plan is part of a designed 'package' then how do we go about ensuring that quality care is 'on offer'? In this section I want to briefly outline some of the indicators by which we may assess the standards of care we purchase or provide for our clients. Much of what I say has been produced by the Social Services Inspectorate teams in their report *Homes are for Living In* (Department of Health, 1989a) and later guidance from them and the Department of Health (1990) (which I found was invaluable when helping an elderly aunt to choose a nursing home which would cater for her needs and strengths). Residential and day-care centres for other client groups equally may have the following criteria applied when assessing for quality assurance purposes. Readers may wish to pursue the organisation and management literature (Social Information Systems, 1990) for a broader analysis of quality assurance.

The main features to look for are:

Choice, the opportunity to select independently from a range of options; sensitivity to ethnic and religious dimensions; the environment, such as choice of furnishings, adaptations, etc.

Rights, for instance in relation to care practices such as handling one's own affairs, confidentiality, respect, consultation.

Independence, including a willingness to accept a degree of calculated risk, such as being able to make meals for oneself and others.

Privacy, recognising the need to be alone, to 'own' a bedroom, to have an opportunity to discuss problems in private.

Dignity, which recognises one's intrinsic value and uniqueness; for example mode of address, access to bathing, sensitivity of admission procedures (see Neill, 1989).

Fulfilment, whereby all aspects of daily life help in realising personal aspirations and abilities.

Each of the above set yardsticks for measuring tangible and intangible elements. An in-depth assessment of the 'fulfilment' criteria would therefore suggest that a good home seeks to:

1. Know what residents have done in their earlier life and the skills and interests retained.
2. Help clients to continue to use such skills if they wish and aspire to new ones.
3. Foster the maintenance of relationships and create conditions for new ones if so desired.
4. Understand and cater for emotional and spiritual needs.
5. Create a lifestyle which is flexible to residents' changing needs.

Putting flesh on other criteria by which to measure quality standards

It is essential that information brochures outline the physical features of the home, the services provided by outside bodies and what they cost, if furniture and pets may be brought in, information on the trial period and the complaints procedure. Before admission, the client and carers need to have their expectations regarding personal care, mealtimes, diet, sleeping arrangements, smoking and use of alcohol norms, medical support, nightstaff support, gender of staff carrying out intimate care, frequency of bedroom cleaning, laundering facilities, and so on, clearly written down and agreed. Any quality assured home will ensure that the individual's service expectations and plan are regularly monitored and reviewed, perhaps by a designated practitioner, who ensures that all the other care staff implement these processes with clients and relatives.

Although many clients and their helpers do not enquire further than this, it behoves those who have case management responsibility for needs and service assessment to explore how staff are recruited, trained and supported. For example, it helps to know which attributes and qualifications are deemed to be crucial; it is informative to ask about staff induction into health and safety procedures, safe lifting techniques and promoting residents' interests, and it is indicative of striving for best practice if regular professional supervision processes permeate the establishment, together with a culture for pursuing and taking pride in superior service.

Case example using two models of assessment

The following referral was analysed by a student in placement, relying on two models of assessment: the first is an adaptation of that suggested by Vickery (1976) while the second utilises systems thinking which maps interactional patterns, i.e. the relationships between the systems involved. (More will be said about this later in Chapter 7.) These were initial assessments, the start of thinking through a situation prior to deciding on appropriate action. The referral came from a volunteer, the latest in a series of visitors, who had called on ninety-year-old Mrs Moore a few times. Mrs Moore lived alone in a sheltered bungalow, visited regularly by her daughter and son-in-law and occasionally by a son who had had to move away to find work. Home help was supplied daily; meals on wheels had stopped as Mrs Moore did not like them. The volunteer was concerned that the home was looking neglected, the client was 'confused' and incontinent and said that her home help spent a lot of time talking to her. The warden's job description limited her involvement to occasional shopping and being 'on call' for emergencies.

Vickery's (1976) unified assessment asks us to take into account the assets and liabilities in the situation at the level of the individual, the group, the neighbourhood, the organisation and the wider environment; she also asks:

1. What are the problems in this situation?
2. Who are the clients (i.e. who will benefit)?
3. What are the goals from each one's perspective?
4. Who or what has to be changed or influenced?
5. What are the tasks and roles of the social worker?

In this instance, the student was working in a health centre as a member of a multidisciplinary team; he was able to draw on their expertise and gain the community's respect with relative ease. Having sought the permission of Mrs Moore (whose health assessment revealed that she was forgetful – not confused, which is a confusing label in itself; the occupational therapist (OT) assessment revealed a broken toilet seat, which could account for some of the incontinence), the student called a meeting of the helping network to the health centre to help Mrs Moore and himself answer the above questions. The home help, daughter, Mrs Moore and the volunteer attended and drew up the assessment shown in Table 1.1. What was interesting was that, normally, these helpers never met one another. This had led to some duplication of effort, miscommunication, distorted perceptions especially about acceptable risk and lack of knowledge of various roles. Sharkey (1989) writes that the size of someone's network is less important than the notion of density, i.e. if people know each other well or not. Following the meeting Mrs Moore's network had changed from a loose-knit to a closer-knit one without involving many new, confusing helpers.

Table 1.1   *Initial assessment*

Definition of the problem	Client	Goals	Target	Role/task of social worker
Mrs M's need for care patterned to her daily needs	Mrs M	Coordinate efforts of helpers Review and develop services	Helpers Services	Coordinator Case manager Networker
Rapid turn-over of volunteers	Mrs M Home help Family Future clients	Persuade voluntary agency to try to match volunteers to client need for stability	Voluntary organisation	Educator Advocate Broker Public Relations
Role of Wardens in housing, i.e. sheltered schemes	Tenants	Liaise with housing welfare department to reconsider policy	Housing	Liaison Negotiator Policy researcher
Need for community care and case management system	Service users	To present own agency and SSD with ideas for case management	Own agency/SSD Rest of multidisciplinary team	Researcher Manager Planner Budgeter
Break up of natural networks and pressure on carers	Natural helpers Future consumers and carers	Explore extent of loss of natural helping networks	Politicians Local decision makers	Campaigner Investigator Community developer

One way of showing this on an assessment form is to use an ecomap to display the interaction between particular systems, in this case Mrs Moore's support network. As shown in Figure 1.1 the density of the elderly person's network increased following the student's problem-solving network meeting, in other words, people who had never met or co-ordinated their efforts began to do so following this initial assessment meeting.

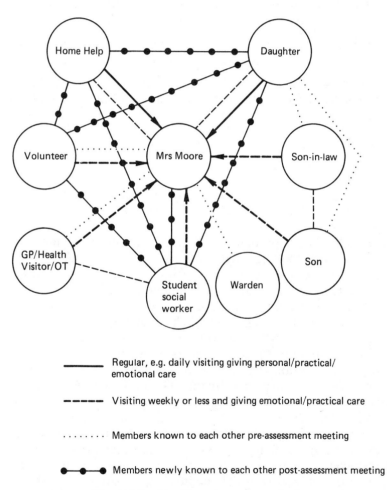

_____ Regular, e.g. daily visiting giving personal/practical/emotional care

- - - - - Visiting weekly or less and giving emotional/practical care

· · · · · · · Members known to each other pre-assessment meeting

●—●—● Members newly known to each other post-assessment meeting

Figure 1.1 *Mrs Moore's support systems*

Finally, before we leave this topic of assessment, it has to be emphasised how careful we have to be when working in arenas such as dementia, not simply because of the need for accurate medical diagnosis, but also because of the runaway spiral which is created when a complaint from a referrer adds to the sufferer's distress, leading to more agitation and withdrawal. This then spirals into depression, the label 'dementia' usually being applied which often results in removal of the person from the community and possible death from the trauma. This negative health cycle from

label → to → dependent sick role → to → diminishing physical, mental and social capacity

is unfortunately too common in the care of elderly people. It is worthwhile consulting the guidelines produced by Marshall (1990) for further advice on this subject.

Record keeping

Although at one time seen as a troublesome chore which reduced the time available for client contact, record keeping is beginning to be recognised as a core skill in which, where possible, clients participate. The record registers significant facts, evidence, feelings, decisions, action taken and planned, monitoring, review, evaluation and costing information. It may take the form of a detailed verbatim account, a concise summary of each incident or contact, a proforma chart on which to tick or highlight coded information, or it may include lengthy social histories, individual programme plans, community profiles, video/audio material or any of the tools mentioned earlier in the assessment section. Sometimes the record, whether in manual or computerised forms, is split into specific sections reflecting the intake, ongoing and ending phases of the work; it may hold letters, medicals, documents from other agencies and, for instance in the event of using a goal-oriented form of practice such as task-centred work (see Chapter 4), contain a working agreement or contract with the client. Here we are talking about formal agency records which are usually confidential, per-

manent and occasionally transferrable to other organisations. (Social workers may make personal records or jottings
which are not official registers of service given.)

Legal enforcement giving clients access to their records
dates mainly from 1984: the data protection law gave
statutory right of access to files held on computer. Since then
the Access to Personal Files Act has extended this to manual
records in housing and social services departments. Thus,
from 1 April 1989 people have had a right to see their
manual records (though there is no legal obligation to show
manual records before that date). Anyone wishing to look at
their files must give notice to the authorities who are allowed
forty days to respond: any information about third parties,
excluding professionals, should not be shown unless they
give consent: pre 1 April 1989 files should block out the
names of such third parties. An approach to good practice is
portrayed by Neville and Beak (1990). They found that
asking clients to countersign their records gave a boost to the
working relationship and enshrined a commitment to consulting the users of our services, i.e. doing with rather than
doing to.

Because of the especial vulnerability of black clients
who are more likely to be discriminated against, Ahmad
(1990) stresses that reports must be accurate, relevant,
portray strengths, address culture in a constructive way and
provide the person or the family with the opportunity to
record their own perspectives. Despite good intentions,
records are highly selective accounts of data remembered
and thought to be significant by the worker.

The primary purpose of keeping records is to improve
service delivery but they can also be used:

- as learning and teaching material
- for supervision purposes
- for administrative purposes, e.g. budgeting
- to ensure accountability
- for research and evaluation
- to illustrate shortfalls or absence of services
- to 'cover' the worker for work done
- to provide continuity when workers change

- to aid planning and decision making
- to monitor progress
- as an *aide mémoire*
- to facilitate client participation, as indicated.

One of the difficulties for beginners is knowing how to confine themselves to needed information; inexperience leads to lengthy records, which cannot be automatically equated with quality data! As a minimum, the record should address the nature of the problem or situation: strengths and resources available and needed, short, medium and long-term goals: plan of action (strategy) and client views.

Before I end this theme, the team who were responsible for developing comunity care case management at the Personal Social Services Research Unit (PSSRU) in Kent have devised a set of documents by which social workers can plot their activities (see Challis and Chesterman, 1985). These consist of four separate items for systematic recording: an Assessment Document, a Monitoring Chart, Periodic Review forms and Costing Information. The Assessment Document was designed to strike a balance between structured precoded information and space for recording individual personal characteristics of each elderly client. Its six sections covered basic details such as age, address, source of referral; formal and informal contacts including inputs from carers and statutory services; housing and financial circumstances with details of heating, toilet and benefits; managing daily living covered key activities such as personal care, night care and household jobs; physical health and mental health in the fifth and sixth parts was concerned with immobility, instability (falling), incontinence, intellectual impairment and the client's attitude to help including informal carers.

The Monitoring Chart consisted of a single sheet showing a matrix of the seven days of the week on the vertical axis and critical periods of the day such as meal-times and bed-time on the horizontal axis: seeing who was meeting needs at various times revealed periods of solitude and risk so that plans could be modified accordingly, especially when the case manager was absent. The chart was left in the client's home so that all involved could communicate and co-ordinate their activities (Challis *et al.*, 1990). Periodic Review forms, while useful say every three months to check the process of care, were found to be more valuable at times of change or crisis: these covered details such as problems and changes achieved; changes intended; social worker activities; outside agencies; practical services and finally resources required but unavailable (which also gave management information about resource deployment).

The fourth document was the Costing Sheet. This recorded expenditure from the social worker's budget used to pay helpers, home help, meals on wheels, day care or residential care. The information was divided into thirteen weekly units; each sheet covering the costing per client over one quarter of the year.

As you can see, these kinds of recording systems could be used in work with other client groups, adapted in relation to particular circumstances and methods of intervention. We can go on now to consider other aspects of case management: counselling, networking and resource mobilisation.

2

Case Management: Counselling, Networking and Mobilising Resources

If case management is to succeed as a strategy for organising and co-ordinating services at the level of the individual client it has to concentrate on the minutiae of interactions between helper and helped. In this, counselling plays a pivotal role. So too do networking and resource mobilisation; these practices will constitute the focus of this chapter.

Counselling

The British Association for Counselling defines 'What is counselling?' as 'when a person, occupying regularly or temporarily the role of counsellor, offers and agrees explicitly to give time, attention and respect to another person, or persons, who will temporarily be in the role of client (*Membership Notes*, 1990). The task is to give the client an opportunity to explore, discover and clarify ways of living more resourcefully and towards greater well-being. This is a very broad description which allows for the fact that counselling has many schools – behavioural, psychodynamic and humanistic (e.g. Transactional Analysis Counselling (Stewart, 1989) as well as feminist and transcultural versions. In this chapter two models of counselling are described, the well-known approaches of Rogers (1980) and those of Egan

(1981). A search of the vast literature will reveal, whatever the school of thought, generically workers need to be able to listen, observe and respond. And yet, this is far from easy: acquiring skills in attending, specifying, confronting, questioning (as we saw in the previous chapter), reflecting feelings and content, personalising, problem solving and action planning, is far from simple, It seems to take years of practice and, in my experience, constant use to prevent these skills becoming 'rusty'. In addition, Nelson-Jones (1983) recommends that to become a skilled counsellor it takes more than being caring and understanding; one has to show this through technical expertness as well. When we examined interviewing in Chapter 1 a critical, prerequisite was the ability to listen, not as a passive act, but as a highly active process paying attention to what is being said and how it is being said, for instance. Furthermore, effective counsellors must own the following seven qualities:

1. *Empathy or understanding,* the effort to see the world through the other person's eyes.
2. *Respect,* responding in a way which conveys a belief in the other's ability to tackle the problem.
3. *Concreteness or being specific*, so that the counsellee can be enabled to reduce confusion about what he/she means.
4. *Self-knowledge and self-acceptance*, ready to help others with this.
5. *Genuineness*, being real in a relationship.
6. *Congruence*, so that the words we use match our body language.
7. *Immediacy*, dealing with what is going on in the present moment of the counselling session, as a sample of what is going on in someone's everyday life.

Books which offer exercises for practice (Corey, 1986) help develop technical expertise. Rather than attempt to do the same here, let us document those microskills which seem to give learners special difficulty and ask readers to identify where they may have limitations and accordingly need to keep practising. I confess my own 'sticking points' at the end of the list!

Are you able to:

Let a person finish talking without reacting?
Accurately reflect back content and feelings?
Paraphrase what someone has said?
Summarise to move interviews forward?
Clarify your own role to the other person?
Use open questions?
Use prompts to encourage the person to continue?
Draw out feelings?
Offer tentative understanding?
Tune into how the other person affects you?
Tolerate silences of about five seconds?
Control your own anxiety and relax?
Focus on the 'here and now' as well as 'there and then'?
Provide direction and keep focus in the session?
Recognise and confront ambivalence and inconsistencies?
Set mutual goals?
Tolerate painful topics?
Discuss and generate alternative plans of action?
Evaluate costs and gains of what was achieved?
Begin, sustain and end well (each session and the whole contact)?

I 'get stuck' with the first two skills, mainly, I think, because in teaching there is scope for giving advice, guidance and information which can get in the way of drawing out what the other person can contribute. Advice and directions are all right, when this is timely and when they are sought. But, in counselling, one's own perspective can truly interfere with the counsellee's journey into self-assessment, self-awareness or self-determination. Whenever we are tempted to begin a sentence with 'I think . . .' or 'My feelings are . . .' it is worth biting one's tongue. By talking about 'me' and 'my' we step outside the other person's frame of reference, which is at the heart of the counselling encounter. In fact, when situations are still being explored no clever responses are called for: maybe all that is needed is to reflect back the other's statements beginning with 'You think . . .' or 'Your feelings are . . .' to *allow people to listen to themselves.*

Workshops to develop counselling skills usually reveal that inexperienced people have a tendency to cover up their uncertainty by trying too hard, interrupting too much (what Jacobs (1985) calls 'having two mouths and one ear') and feeling responsible for someone else's difficulties. Unhelpful tendencies appear too, such as preaching, falsely reassuring, judging and offering unasked for interpretations (another of my peccadillos until pointed out to me). In sum, we are never helpful when we do not allow the other person to be different from oneself. Self-monitoring, live supervision or peer counselling could be useful ways of changing habits.

Other factors which could affect counselling relationships and which might be mentioned are those of disability, class, gender and race differences. If counselling relies so much on understanding the client's experience and frame of reference then where the therapist comes from a different background it might be assumed that empathic understanding is not possible. There are problems with this assumption. For instance, white social workers could become blinkered by the issue of a so-called black culture, feeling deskilled by a lack of knowledge of religious beliefs and daily living habits. As Ahmad (1990) points out, how relevant is the aspect of the client's culture to the needs of the client and the nature of the counselling interaction? Do we check the cultural realities of all our clients? How do we guard against oversimplistic explanations which ignore underlying emotional (and, indeed, stuctural) factors which, for example, contribute to someone's depression? In interpersonal contacts where the worker is white and the client black while both are aware of this significant factor both participants possibly agree to a conspiracy of silence, the worker feeling guilty about being the 'oppressor'. Or, assuming that being black is a disadvantage, could result in ignoring clients' strengths. The major elements in counselling, particularly Rogers' 'client-centred' approach, which aimed to facilitate the self-actualising potential of people, was really about equalising the distribution of power. This requires white workers accepting clients correcting their preconceptions and being open to confrontation, e.g. that they could never know what it is like to live continually with rejection, humiliation and discrimination, which can so undermine self-respect.

Black workers similarly may feeling uncomfortable with white clients, concerned that they will never be able to understand the others' realities. If both worker and client are black this could create barriers to openness and self-disclosure if the client believes that the worker has 'sold out' to the establishment or if the worker overidentifies because of the common bond of racial experience. On the other hand, beneficial counselling opportunities exist when white clients welcome the chance to share feelings of exploitation with black helpers or when a black counsellor's positive self-concept (Maximé, 1986) offers a sense of hope to the black client.

Having said this, though, the very notion of counselling as a model of helping, developed according to Western values, beliefs and perspectives could be inappropriate to immigrant groups such as Asian Indians, Chinese and Vietnamese people. For instance, the concepts of self-determination, individualisation, independence and self-disclosure may conflict with values such as interdependence, acceptance and self-control. Because of this some writers (Hirayama and Cetingok, 1988) favour empowerment of the family or whole community rather than focus on an individual: goals would then reflect loyalty, solidarity and cooperation, the worker taking a more active role as teacher, resource consultant and mediator.

In relation to gender differences, feminist literature has stressed that women clients should be seen by female therapists as only women can understand women (there is some acknowledgement, however, that feminist counselling currently does not incorporate black perspectives and is somewhat middle-class-bound (Dominelli and McLeod, 1989)). The evidence seems to indicate that counsellors – both male and female – are affected by prevailing sex-role stereotyping (about men and women) (see Hall, 1987). Thus Hall (1987) points out that, amongst other changes, practice should address the allocation of workers to clients as an important issue in establishing a relationship. So, we know that in the initial stages of counselling women who have been beaten, raped or subject to incest there is a preference for women counsellors; but later, the female client may gain more from a male counsellor who provides a different role model. The research into gender matching and matching client and worker more generally is at times contradictory and inconclusive, but should not be ignored for all that. It would be a backward step to be sexist by omission. The literature quoted here is an introduction to looking at this phenomenon in more depth.

I would add that another group for whom counselling is just as important are those who are elderly. Too frequently we assume that problems occur merely because of old age rather than the unique conflicts which face each of us at any age. Ageism makes us fail to see when older people are depressed, abusing alcohol and drugs, having sexual problems, wanting to develop self-awareness or trying to modify behaviour and attitudes. A fruitful book is that by Scrutton (1989).

To move on now to the actual theory and methods of counselling, taking first Carl Rogers' humanistic approach to client-centred (also called person-centred) counselling.

Two counselling models

Carl Rogers, who died in 1987, developed client-centred therapy which implied that those who sought help were responsible people with power to direct their own lives: in fact, he had originally called his approach 'Non-Directive therapy' but later was convinced that there is a tendency towards growth and change, and that, given the right climate in the therapeutic relationship, people can discover and direct their personal power. Rogers' whole attitude was grounded in the belief that the client is the only natural authority about her or himself; he trusted human beings to be able to move towards constructive growth with the help of a worker who demonstrated empathy, congruence and positive regard. Thus, the counsellor does not know best and cannot operate in a superior or expert way. As Rogers hoped, his ideas continue to develop, though there is a danger seen by some (Merry, 1990) that therapists might start to trust their techniques more than they trust their clients.

The goal of this approach is the greater integration and independence of the individual: the focus is on the person rather than on solving the presenting problem. Through the counsellor's attitudes of genuine caring, respect and understanding, people are able to loosen their defences and open themselves to new experiences and revised perceptions. As the helping relationship progresses clients are able to express deeper feelings such as shame, anger and guilt, previously deemed too frightening to incorporate into their sense of self.

Frequently, people come to us in a state of incongruence; there is a discrepancy between how they see themselves (self-concept) and how they would like to see themselves (ideal self-concept). Or, as in the case example below, a contrast exists between self-concept and experience in reality. In the interview the worker is helping Linda to explore her sense of who she is, separate from the feedback which she apparently receives from those in her environment. This conflict, about the way we are and the way we want to be or the way we feel we are compared to what others say we are is sometimes at the root of all sorts of problems. While assenting that busy social service agencies may not have the time to let clients peel away the layers of their difficulties so as to work things out for themselves, it would be short-sighted to overlook the value of motivating clients towards self-management; it can help prevent problems worsening and can reduce the need to return to our departments again and again.

Case example

Linda is sixteen, living at home with her mother who is a single parent. There are two older children, grown up and living away from home. Linda attends the local Further Education college, studying a business course. She calls in the office of social services to ask for help, desperate because her mother is asking for help with the housework as she too works outside the home. Yet this leaves little time for Linda to study for her exams which are looming. In general, without an efficient duty system and easy access to the department, the client would be redirected to seek help from a student counsellor (assuming one exists). Although allocated low priority this is the kind of referral which, with minimum but sufficient attention, could prevent more serious difficulties later. Respecting the client's wishes, no contact with anyone else is planned at this stage.

The transcript is taken from the first interview, in the first half hour. The client unloads all of her mixed-up feelings towards her mother, but really towards her *self*. Her mother, burdened by her own duties, tells Linda that she is selfish and lazy: adolescents in particular seem to internalise others' opinions (Noonan, 1983) which can result in confusion about differentiating between 'me' and 'not me' phenomena.

L (despairingly) I can't do anything to please my mum.
C How does that make you feel?
L (after a pause) I don't know.
C You look sad about it.
L Well, it makes me feel miserable . . . (struggling).
C . . . Not knowing what pleases your mum?
L Nothing I do pleases her.
C Are you saying that the things you do for your mother are not appreciated? Is that what makes you feel miserable?
L I just wish she'd stop picking on me. I'd do anything for her but she only wants it done in her time.
C Can you give me an example of something that has happened this week?
L This morning she asked me to do the breakfast dishes. I was late for 'Tech' and said I'd do them when I got home. But she ranted and raved so I had to do them then.
C You sound angry about that.
L I think she is being unreasonable.
C (neutral tone) You feel *you're* not unreasonable.

L   *She* says I am.
C   What do you think?
L   About not doing the dishes?
C   Yes. Do you feel that you are unreasonable as a person?
L   I don't know.

Often people who seek help feel a great deal of ambivalence towards significant others in their lives; in Linda's case, she feels only conditional acceptance that she is a 'good' person in her interactions with her mother. Because the counsellor is wise and mature no sides are taken and no blame attached to anyone as this would detract from the aim to help the youngster work through a reflective re-cognition (recognition) of herself. The counsellor realises too that counselling is a two-way process where worker and client need to take each other into account: at times we overlook how much clients affect our feelings (Kell and Mueller, 1966).

Framework for understanding counselling

To give a framework now which summarises Rogers' *client-centred approach* (1980):

Theory base and important concepts devolve from a philosophical background of the existential tradition which respects an individual's subjective experience and places emphasis on the vocabulary of freedom, choice, autonomy and meaning. It is a humanistic approach which is concerned with growth and 'becoming', recognising the importance of the self-concept and the potential for self-actualisation, i.e. a 'fully functioning person'. Given appropriate nurturing conditions such as authentic, warm, empathic, unconditional relationships with significant others, people automatically grow in positive ways. It forms a 'third force' theoretical alternative to the psychoanalytic and behavioural approaches considered in Chapters 5 and 6. The theory also draws on phenomenological perspectives – the way in which a person's experience of their self is congruent or otherwise with the way they 'experience their self in the world'.

Problems which arise include psychological disturbance owing to the inner conflict between self-experience and the way one is perceived by others: conditional acceptance from important relationships puts limits on the extent to which one can really be oneself.

Goals of therapy are to assist someone in their growth process; to help an individual become a fully functioning person by openness to experience and ambiguity, self-trust, developing an internal source of evaluation and learning that growth and revision are ongoing processes, not once-and-for-all end products of therapy.

The client's role is to move away from 'oughts' and 'shoulds', that is, living up to the expectations of others. A person decides their own standards and independently validates the choices and decisions which are made. In a climate of acceptance clients have the opportunity to experience the whole range of their feelings thereby becoming less defensive about their hidden, negative aspects. They develop 'a way of being'. (At times, clients are instrumental in helping counsellors develop away from 'doing something' into 'being there' for others as Bhaduri's (1990) account of work with the Rahman family showed.)

The worker's role and techniques. Rogers' views gradually shifted away from techniques towards the personhood of the worker and the therapeutic relationship which communicated acceptance, respect, understanding and sharing. The counsellor does not use techniques in the creation of an accepting climate as this would depersonalise the encounter and the counsellor would not be genuine. In some ways this approach has built-in safety features for novices who do not have to offer interpretations and the like: staying within the other's frame of reference offers some assurance that clients will not be harmed by this caring approach which thereby encourages the client to care for her/his self.

Another model of counselling, which counteracts some of the limitations of the above when counsellors listen and reflect but do not challenge, is the three-stage approach attributed to Egan (1981). He has recently extended the three stages of *Exploration*, *Understanding* and *Action* to a fourth stage of *Evaluation*. Each of these stages is diagrammatically represented by four adjacent diamond shapes; these signify the widening and narrowing of focus within each interview and along the total helping process. Accordingly, following a wide exploration of the problem, based on the foundation of a relationship of trust and mutual endeavour, the counsellor helps the counsellee to narrow down their discussion so that an assessment can be formulated. Following this, enquiry opens up again so that the client and helper can gain an understanding and maybe a new perspective on the difficulties. This reveals which goals to aim for but, in order to consider a range of alternative change strategies, the interview has to be wide-ranging again, prior to focusing down later on a specific plan of action. Finally, a broad-ranging discussion opens up as a way of evaluating, 'how did it go?' before closer examination of the chosen problem-solving method is undertaken. Then if necessary in a circular fashion, the first stage of wide exploration is resumed as part of the helping process. Some skills which can be used in each stage are as follows:

Stage 1: exploration skills. The worker aims to establish rapport, assisting in the exploration of thoughts, feelings and behaviour relevant to the problem in hand. Asking, 'What is the difficulty?' the counsellor tries to build trust and a working alliance, using active listening, reflecting, paraphrasing and summarising skills. Open questions are used before the client is asked to say which concrete problem they and the helper need to understand.

Stage 2: understanding skills. The counsellor continues to be facilitative, using Stage 1 skills and in addition helps the person to piece together the picture that has emerged. Themes and patterns may be pointed out to assist in gaining new perspectives: this alternative point of view aids clearer understanding of what the person's goals are and identifies strengths and resources. The skills lie in offering an alternative frame of reference, using disclosure of oneself appropriately, staying in touch with what is happening here-and-now and using confrontation. This latter skill is not to be misunderstood as an attack. It is an act of caring, of encouraging clients to consider what they are doing or not doing, challenging inconsistencies and conflicting ideas in order to tap the person's unused resources. Egan would view confrontation without support as disastrous and support without confrontation as anaemic. The timing of confrontation is vital when the relationship can endure such a challenge.

Stage 3: action skills. The worker and the counsellee begin to identify and develop resources for resolving or coping with the causes of concern, based on a thorough understanding of self and situation. The skills lie in setting goals, providing support and resources, teaching problem solving if necessary, agreeing purposes and using decision-making abilities.

Stage 4: evaluation. An action plan having been chosen and tried, all ideas are reviewed and measured for effectiveness. The counsellor's skills rely again on active listening plus all those of the previous stages.

As you can see, the worker's use of influence and expert authority is acknowledged in Egan's approach which contrasts with what was said about the Rogerian school of thought. Not all clients are willing ones; in social service and probation departments, despite critical argument (see Rojek *et al.,* 1988), whether we admit it or not, we act as agents of control. Even when help is sought, there is natural resistance to dependency and the power of professionals. Social workers use authority which stems from their statutory powers, their position in an organisation as well as the authority which derives from their knowledge and skill. Apart from abuse of power, supposedly anathema in our profession but not unheard of, authority can be used in counselling for setting limits, just as staff in Intermediate Treatment projects do to help teenage offenders to gain control over themselves. Equally, we gain authority on occasion from the strength of our relationships and skills in persuading and negotiating, Yet, it needs to be remembered that in using all kinds of authority, we are only as powerful as others allow us to be: influence has to be validated by others. There are ways, furthermore, of sharing power with users by explaining the skills and techniques which are used, for instance in counselling and networking, dealt with in a moment. The case study in the previous chapter was one example of this, when the student brought together members of an elderly person's network to illustrate how the label of dementia can get out of hand. A further example of partnership was a project set up to help long-term clients, demeaned as 'problem families', to become competent, not merely in running their own lives again, but in taking over the management committee and budgeting of a Family Centre set up originally to help them in traditional ways (Benn, 1981).

Networking

I want to say a little more about the practice of networking especially as it has become a popular concept with various disciplines in recent times. Here I will analyse three separate strategies.

1. *Network therapy*. This is a therapeutic approach where network assemblies, using techniques drawn from large groupwork, help families in crisis by bringing together their network to act as the change agents; the case example is of a network assembly (see Rueveni, 1979).

2. *Problem-solving network meetings*. These bring together formal and informal carers as we have seen; they are useful when unravelling non-complementary professional networks in order to sort out who is doing what (see Dimmock and Dungworth, 1985).

3. *Network construction*. This method aims to sustain, change and build new networks. Used originally to help those with chronic schizophrenia whose institutionalisation had led to the loss of their networks, we see network building used extensively nowadays in keeping elderly people in the community (Challis *et al.*, 1990) and to engage supporters for those with learning disabilities (Atkinson, 1986).

A network assembly

Bringing together a 'tribal' gathering to act as change agent for a family member in crisis was devised by Speck (1967). He recognised the loneliness of people who keep problems to themselves or receive help from large, impersonal organizations. Therefore, with an individual's permission, he invited the network to one or two 'healing ceremonies': any household members, active and passive relatives, friends and neighbours, contacts from work, leisure, places of worship and those who knew of the person were asked to contribute to working out ways of helping at a time of great need. These full-scale assemblies often resulted in up to fifty people attending. Partial network assemblies (Van der Velden *et al.*, 1984) have since simplified the procedure, using fewer participants of about a dozen people.

The referral is taken by a team of three or four social workers who know and respect each other's work. A preliminary assessment interview with significant members ensures that an assembly is appropriate and that everyone understands what will happen. The family is asked to invite about twelve contacts to their home; they are coached in how to do this and how to explain that the purpose is to get the benefit of everyone's ideas. The balance of the group is important. Each core member needs to have one ally, someone as a supporter to prevent scapegoating and promote compassion. Representatives from the close and distant zones around the family's world allows peripheral people, who have no axe to grind, to provide different perspectives, a range of solutions and possibly increased energy to help with the emotional and practical issues which are raised. The skilled team hope to exploit the 'network effect', which is the result of simply bringing people together.

The stages of helping begin with convening the network, moving towards connecting members with one another ('retribalisation'), then shifting responsibility for solutions from the team to the natural group. Customarily, an introduction exercise is used to help people to relax. One social worker acts as the conductor while the rest act as group facilitators. Everyone listens as those central to the referral put their view of the problem.

Lists of complaints are transformed into goals for change, then the outsiders are asked for their solutions. Normally, polarised opinions and ideas emerge; the team use this energy to mobilise people towards alterations: activists within the group help to shift the meeting from depression at what seems unalterable towards breakthrough when solutions and offers of support develop. At this point of 'exhaustion/elation' the professional team leave.

These innovations have helped families facing bereavement, disability, suicide attempts, alcoholism and drug addiction and other 'hopeless' situations, reminding participants that others do care and that friends and neighbours still rally around in desperate times. Ballard and Rosser (1979) write about a family who were subject to violent attacks from their daughter Christine, aged eighteen. Following her discharge from a psychiatric hospital they met 35 members of the family's network: this was really a full-scale assembly needing the space of the local vicarage. Christine's network varied in their reactions to her 'crazy' behaviour, but after venting their anger they then became depressed that they had not helped more. Problem solving in small groups, the assembly produced offers of assistance with accommodation, transport, employment and renewed contact with the family. At a follow-up meeting, no tangible support had been given but the family were less bothered about this aspect than their relief at being reconnected to their support network.

A problem-solving network meeting

This form of networking is, in essence, a straightforward negotiation session, developed by Garrison and Howe (1976). It is now commonly used by professional networks who, in the process of helping, have become stuck and who need to clarify their respective roles and responsibilities. The meeting is a structured one, where each participant in turn might be asked, 'What is the problem?'; 'What has been tried so far?'; 'How can agency personnel help?' and 'What goal can everyone agree to work towards?'. Thus, in this form of networking, the purpose of the meeting and the time available for it need to be clearly stated. Everyone needs to have the opportunity to state their position and plan; then specific tasks are delegated. Usually, a follow-up meeting is needed (about three weeks later) to ensure that agreements are working.

Carpenter and Treacher (1989) discuss 'agency triangles' when clients or agencies triangulate a spectrum of other agencies so that no-one is sure who is the 'customer' anymore. Disputes between inter-agency networks rage as much as they do in the referred problem; passing the buck and arguing about who 'should' do what unfortunately is becoming a major issue for those involved in monitoring complex cases. The following example shows some of this.

Case example

John was a thirty-year-old man with learning disabilities. He lived with his brother and sister-in-law and attended the local Adult Training Centre where the rest of the trainees' needs were more involved than his own. John started stealing and according to the Training Centre manager this was due to the environment being insufficiently challenging. The client was put on probation and the officer duly arranged for him to attend a Life Skills course at a college in the town. John refused to attend and his family insisted that he return to the Adult Training Centre.

When the client, his family, the centre manager, probation officer and the case manager met to rethink the 'package' of care, their meeting was chaired by a team leader who was independent of the case. It became clear that all the agencies were working on what they thought was good for John, without consulting him or his family about *their* choices. It transpired that they were quite happy with the Training Centre; John, in particular, did not want to lose contact with his friends there, whom he had begun to miss.

The network meeting revealed different viewpoints and some misunderstandings about the philosophies of each agency; the users of the service were given the chance to hear these views and put forward their own.

A network construction

This involves the social worker coaching someone in how to sustain, build or change their network. First, the person is helped to draw a network or ecomap (see Figure 2.1). As was mentioned earlier in Chapter 1 when discussing assessment, a sheet with many circles is used to represent the household itself, neighbours, general practitioner, school, clubs, shop, work and so on. The network map is filled in using the same colour to connect who knows whom: relationships between the client and others which are strong, weak or stressful are depicted by different symbols.

Secondly, the person is helped to assess from this the sources of interference and intimacy and, if appropriate, asked if they wish to lessen or strengthen these bonds. Thirdly, overlooked sources of help are examined, with the client and worker planning how these could be developed: this is a form of resource mobilisation to which we shall come presently.

Case example

Mrs Young was a thirty-five-year-old woman with one son, Paul aged twelve years. She had recently divorced her husband, who had access to his son at weekends. Mrs Young had come to the UK from Germany fifteen years previously and although living on a busy council estate knew very few people. She applied to the large Voluntary Society to become a foster parent to an older child. The worker from the Placement Team helped Mrs Young to map her network; as you can see from Figure 2.1 (and comparing it possibly to your own), the client had a small and not very active network to whom she could turn for support. Some members had strong ties but the client agreed that she was isolated and had wanted a companion for Paul. Mrs Young had stopped writing to her own family in Germany: the worker encouraged her to rebuild these links which she did, eventually being visited by them. Paul's school taught evening-classes in German where, in time, Mrs Young began to help students there. She withdrew her application to foster.

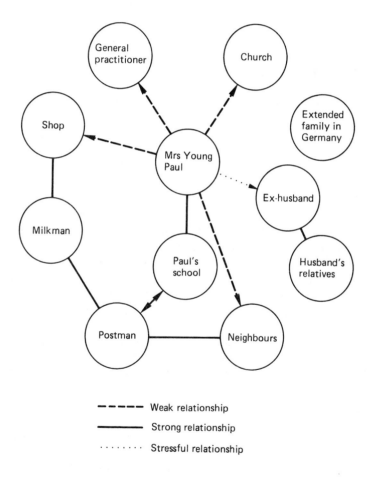

------ Weak relationship

------ Strong relationship

········ Stressful relationship

Figure 2.1 *Network map*

Network strategies are starting to provide exciting solutions, for instance in community care schemes to sustain and nurture helpers. (On the other hand, undoing the original support network, encouraging friends and relatives to withdraw when they are under severe stress, has been important too (Challis *et al.*, 1990). So-called 'toxic' networks, for example those of people involved in criminal activities, similarly may need to be loosened.) These practices provide 'people muscle', unite and reunite networks and give back the chance to show concern for others in a non-bureaucratic way.

Mobilising resources

If we were to sit down and calculate how much time social workers relate to people other than their clients, we would come up with a figure of about one third in face-to-face client work, the rest spent in intra-organisational and inter-organisational communications. A great deal of this effort is connected to mobilising resources. This 'hidden face' (Bar-On, 1990) of social work practice will inevitably loom larger as the practice of case management strengthens and when our departments might control less of the resources which clients require. Bar-On's (1990) study concluded that it is inevitable that social workers will have significant contact with other systems on whom they will be functionally dependent – we shall always be requesting something of somebody.

So, what are the practice skills required for indirect activities? Amongst others are negotiation, bargaining, resolving conflicts, mediation, liaison, planning, advocacy, consultation, setting up new projects and co-ordinating resource provision. A book which spells out how to identify, create and interweave resources, alongside discussion of all the above skills, is that by Payne (1986) which is recommended: my own discussion on the practitioner–manager role (1990) is also relevant.

Let us take just one of these skills, negotiation, which is really about influencing in order to get a just outcome;

thereby, negotiation can be both competitive and collaborative (Payne, 1986). Where the social worker is having to fight to secure justice or combat the abuse of power, perhaps by a higher authority, then competitive tactics are in order. Where parties are negotiating towards agreement rather than to gain advantage then collaborative elements are to the fore. In both instances, however, it is important not to lose one's temper but to use anger constructively and not to stray from the point but to keep in focus each part of the bargaining process. Incidentally, anyone who has reared children will see that they have been negotiating all the time; equally, many of the skills of daily practice are about negotiation whether this concerns welfare rights work, persuading schools to cope with disruptive pupils, inducing policy-makers to fund new projects or helping to resolve staff disputes in day and residential centres. Thus, many of the abilities we have already can be relied on in becoming a skilled negotiator. There are a growing number of publications, in the management field and elsewhere, which address this subject: they ordinarily suggest the following ideas.

Negotiating for agreement relies on:

- good preparation, i.e. knowing what you want to achieve, having the facts and planning priorities
- creating a cooperative climate
- agreeing the purpose and procedures for any contact
- exploring via *brief* opening statements your understanding of the situation, your aims, priorities and contribution so that there is seen to be joint advantage
- listening, clarifying and summarising what the other party's opening statement seems to say
- generating creative, interdependent suggestions and then deciding which of these are realistic possibilities
- agreeing on the action necessary to achieve mutual interest.

Negotiating to get justice may involve having to fight for resources, getting the best deal for one's clients by:
- preparation as before, but being more specific about what one is bidding for and not being prepared to be exploited by power games such as giving to get something, appeals

to higher authority, being deflected by numerous questions or dominated by angry outbursts or red-herrings
- creating a climate of goodwill
- exploring in a probing way what is important to the other
- reaching agreements on a broad front before tackling the
detail of what your are asking for
- being prepared to make compromises if this does not
involve loss of integrity and equity
- remaining task-focused rather than attacking someone's
personality.

Case example

Paula was referred anonymously by her neighbours who
complained that her children were at risk, being brought up
in a house which was used by drug addicts, dossers and other
down-and-outs. Before the social worker could visit, the
police became involved and insisted that the children be
taken from their mother. When seen in her home, Paula was
indeed at the mercy of delinquent groups, who exploited her
limited intelligence, refusing to move out until forced to do
so by the police. In the meantime her home had been
wrecked, savage dogs had ripped up most of her furniture
and other belongings. The crisis was so severe that, coupled
with her lack of social skills, Paula was quite unable to
discuss her situation with the social worker, despite the
latter using various communication approaches to help the
woman tell her story.

The social worker used all her powers of persuasion to
make the two policemen who were at the house let her help
the client without resorting to the need to receive the
children into care. She bravely asked for their help to deal
with the dogs and later to take some of Paula's belongings in
their panda car to a homeless families' unit, where Paula and
her children were to stay until the social worker could
negotiate alternative housing with the housing department.

This goal of rehousing demanded the most careful of
preparation, especially as Paula lived in the district's worst
quarter, where the poorest tenants were housed until they

'proved' to the housing department that they were 'fit-enough people' to be transferred into less temporary property. Knowing it was politic, the social worker did not make the mistake of attacking council policy or of challenging the attitudes of housing personnel. She presented a clear, well-thought-through plan for preventing Paula and her children needing to be kept in the homeless unit; the offer of another house, though not much of an improvement on the former, was a start, from which longer-term work with the client, whose husband had recently left her, could begin. All this time too, the social worker had to negotiate with her own department and other agencies who were concerned at Paula's capacity for good-enough parenting. Again, influencing and negotiating with integrity, listening to other points of view and not resorting to pushing people to see her point of view, together with a business-like and confident attitude, helped. Wisely using supervision, she checked tht she was being realistic, asking her senior to give a second opinion on the social work assessment that, once out of the noxious network, and helped to form new ones, Paula had the potential to cope.

Finally, it is as well to remember when we are advocating, liaising and bargaining with resource controllers on whom we might be dependent that within our present hierarchical structures often decisions about the nature and quantity of services are already made (in other words, non-negotiable). At the levels at which most practitioners operate there may be little scope for maneouvrability, and yet, with the introduction of case management and devolved budget arrangements, together with staff on the front line learning organisation and management skills, we could be in a better position to improve resource mobilisation. Moreover, by becoming informed and resourced ourselves, we may be in a better position to improve client choice. Certainly, this might have been one of the aims behind the projects which developed locally-based teams (Bayley *et al.*, 1987). This said, these 'empowering' projects are still grappling with questions related to statutory duties and control of services by local people; whether participation applies to service users only or by other people who live locally; the worry of delegating powers and duties to those who do not have to be held accountable, as well as the complexity of managing joint health and social welfare services. Nevertheless, as Bayley and his colleagues state:

> As greater emphasis is placed upon voluntary and informal care, it seems right that local people should be given a greater part to play in the management of services. Only so will services be able to develop the necessary sensitivity to local need, awareness of the extent of local resources and the ways in which these needs can best be met and the resources tapped appropriately and without being exploitative. (p.18)

3

Crisis Intervention

In this chapter I explore what is meant by the word 'crisis', as it relates to a proper social work approach. Brief case examples are used to clarify the distinction between crises and emergencies and to offer as role models practitioners who were able to 'stand still', that is remain calm, in the face of such situations. The stages of crisis resolution, the signs and symptoms to look for and the difference between stress and crisis are noted. A framework which summarises the main ideas of the approach is followed by a detailed description of the techniques which may be used in the initial, continuing and closing phases of intervention. Related literature associated with disasters, catastrophe and bereavement is introduced; increasingly such incidents have stirred agencies to set up co-ordinated after-care systems and preventive intervention services.

What do we mean by 'crisis'?

Social work interventions repeatedly occur with clients in crisis, and yet the word is generally misunderstood and used in something of a dragnet fashion, indefinitely describing a variety of problems, needs, stress and emergency states. Teams talk about crises when they mean that an urgent referral has come in or that they can only 'do crisis work', that is engage in minimal activity because of overwork. This signifies a lack of understanding of the concept of crisis and methods of intervention: inaccurate use of the term may have actually prevented a more thorough testing of the model such that we cannot yet dignify the crisis approach with the status of 'theory'. It is hoped that, having read this, the reader will avoid uncritical and undifferentiated use of the concept so as correctly to understand, apply and develop the processes.

Nevertheless defining crisis *is* difficult (O'Hagan, 1986), hampered further by the lay-person's portrayal of crisis as a drama, panic, chaos, the 'economic crisis' and so on. The concept of crisis was formulated chiefly by Erich Lindemann and Gerald Caplan who in the 1940s and the 1950s studied the ways in which individuals react to psychologically hazardous situations: for our purposes, therefore, we can accept the definition provided by their student Lydia Rapoport who suggests that *'a crisis is an upset in a steady state'* (Rapoport, 1970, p. 276).

This is a simple way of portraying how a sense of loss associated with accidental or life transitions throws an individual into a state of helplessness, where coping strategies are no longer successful in mastering problems and where the person's psychological defences are weakened. The steady state (also called 'homeostasis' or 'equilibrium') is maintained by human beings through a series of adaptations and problem solving processes – Charles Darwin might have expressed this as a biological survival mechanism since new solutions are usually needed to manage the hazardous event which precipitated such disequilibrium. Crises are not necessarily unusual or tragic events, they can form a normal part of our development and maturation. What happens in crisis is that our habitual strengths and ways of coping do not work; we fail to adjust either because the situation is new to us, or it has not been anticipated, or a series of events become too overwhelming.

If a human being is overpowered by external, interpersonal or intrapsychic forces (in other words, conflicting needs) then harmony is lost for a time. One important thing to remember is that crises are self-limiting, they also have a beginning, middle and end; Caplan (1964) postulated that this period lasts for up to six weeks. In the initial phase there is a rise in tension as a reaction to the impact of stress; during this time habitual ways of trying to solve problems are called on. If this first effort fails this makes tension rise even further as the person gets upset at their ineffectiveness. This state of mind results in the final phase when either the problem is solved or the individual, needing to rid themselves of the problem, redefines it for instance as something less threatening; or, alternatively, the problem is avoided altogether, for example by distancing oneself from it. (The same phenomenon of protest, despair and detachment is familiar to workers who understand the separation trauma of young children.) It can be seen that crises have a peak or turning-point; as this peak approaches, tension mounts and energy for coping is mobilised – we 'rise to the occasion' (Parad and Caplan, 1965, p. 57).

As indicated, during the disorganised recovery stage people are more receptive to being helped because they are less defensive and need to restore the predictability of their worlds. We all seek some kind of balance in our daily lives. Having said this, there are some families and clients who seem to thrive on living in a constant state of crisis; they lurch from one appalling state of chaos to another, on the precipice of eviction, fuel disconnection, abandonment and despair. Unfortunately, this chronic state may be part of the lifestyle and not to be confused with concepts of crisis discussed so far. Later, in Chapter 5, some methods of helping continually disorganised people, whose disasters seem to flow into one another in circular patterns which can almost be predicted, are discussed.

Crises can be perceived as either a threat, a loss or a challenge: the threat can be one to one's self-esteem or to one's sense of trust, for instance; the loss might be an actual one or may be an inner feeling of emptiness and isolation; when viewed as a challenge, a crisis can encompass not only danger but also an opportunity for growth. This is especially so when new methods of solving problems are found or when the person finds that they can cope. Similarly, because crises can revive old, unresolved issues from the past, they can add to the sense of being overwhelmed and over-burdened (a double dose); at the same time however they can offer a second chance to correct non-adjustment to a past event. A couple of case examples will illustrate this vulnerability which runs alongside increased mental energy made available for coping when no longer being used to repress ill-resolved old problems.

Two case examples

1. Mrs Todd was admitted to an elderly persons' home following the death of her husband and at the request of her daughter, aged seventy, who could no longer manage. Six months after admission Mrs Todd refusd to get out of bed for a week saying that there was no point. Physical explanations were ruled out. Sensitive questioning by the residential social worker revealed that the woman had never come to terms with the loss of her husband. On top of this she had been unable to put into words her feelings of being abandoned by her family. The client's denial of her grief, plus the perception that she had lost control and independence (the home was actually run on the high quality standards outlined in Chapter 1) had resulted in confused thinking, distortion of grief and withdrawal.

2. The ward sister of a nearby hospital contacted the field social worker who had spent some months working intensively with the Smith family in order to plan the return home of the Smith's nine-year-old daughter who had become disabled following a road accident. Adaptations and equipment were installed in the home and community care services organised. On being given a definite discharge date, perhaps the first impact of reality, Mr Smith had become uncontrollably tearful, refusing to take his young child home saying that he could not cope. In working through this period of crisis, the social worker helped Mr Smith to 'think straight', to recognise his emotional outpourings as normal and to explore all the resources which would be made available. This little bit of help, given at the right time, prevented Mr Smith from drifting into worries that the family would be abandoned once the little girl was home. In fact, the specificity of a discharge date had triggered off inner conflicts in Mr Smith, only partially resolved, that his wife would leave him, as she had done many years before.

Rather than seek help with their unhappy marriage, the couple had resigned themselves to their disappointment in each other, never talking about the past and trying to pretend that their problems had never existed. In order to uncouple the symbolic links between past and present needs and fears, the social worker re-negotiated her agreement with the Smiths; following short-term crisis intervention a longer term, more open-ended approach to marital counselling was offered.

Neither of these referrals would have been high priority on many caseload weightings; they were not the stuff of drama or danger. A 'fire-fighting' response was not called for and yet these clients were in crisis. They perceived themselves as having no autonomy or mastery over their problems, tension had mounted and thinking had become disintegrated so that little mental energy was left over to use inner and outer resources. Without help, either of these clients could have deteriorated into a major state of personality and behavioural pathology – what is commonly termed a 'nervous breakdown' could have occurred when magical thinking such as 'if I don't think about it the problem will disappear', could have led to a loss of touch with reality or a serious medical condition (a broken heart?).

To sum up, before we compare stress with crisis and learn to recognise the signs of someone in crisis: crises occur throughout life, they are not illnesses; we constantly make adaptive manoeuvres in order to cope and maintain our steady state. But if we meet a novel situation, experience too many life events, or become overloaded with old, unresolved conflicts, then a crisis occurs. This is a time-limited process during which we become disorganised in thinking and behaving. Mounting tension can result in the generation of mental energy for getting the problem solved. Crises can be perceived as a threat, a loss or a challenge; the concept encompasses danger together with opportunity: improved mental health can be the outcome when new methods of coping are found or when there is a second chance to tackle an earlier hazardous event. Equally, the outcome of the crisis can depend on the quality of the person's social support network (Parry, 1990).

Crisis and stress

Occasionally, the word 'stress' is used interchangeably with crisis. However, the concept of stress tends to evoke only negative connotations, for instance that stress is a burden or a load under which people can crack. In comparison, we have seen that the state of crisis need not have this harmful outcome. Crisis contains a growth-promoting possibility; it can be a catalyst, raising the level of mental health by changing old habits of problem solving and evolving new ways of coping. In addition, the concept of stress carries within it a sense of longer-term pressures, which may largely derive from external pressure as opposed to internal conflict. Crisis, on the other hand, appears as a short-term phenomenon where the individual rapidly tries to re-establish previous harmony. Earlier levels of functioning may have been inadequate, but that is where the person's perception of equanimity lay: where crisis resolution is less than optimum then lower levels of coping may result.

Nevertheless, there is a relationship between life events and stress as research shows (Schless *et al.*, 1977). A state of crisis can occur when making social readjustments such as moving house, having a first child, becoming unemployed etc. What is important is that what constitutes unbearable stress for one person may not be so for another. Students are always surprised when they compare their views of stressful events with their colleagues; some dread Christmas, others lose their sense of coping when faced with academic work. Thus, it is the *meaning* which people attach to these 'uneventful' events which matters – maybe someone links Christmas symbolically to an unsatisfactory time in the past; or someone whose self-esteem was bound up with academic success attaches great significance to results. The same is true when we meet clients; what the event means to them is what matters, not whether we think it is serious or not.

Anyone working in the mental health field should be interested in discriminating between stress and crisis. Specifically, when working in crisis intervention mental health teams, where there is a request for compulsory removal to hospital or other safe place, it is vital that a correct assessment is made. Where the client is black, disturbing evidence has emerged of stress being misinterpreted as madness: the rate of admission to psychiatric hospitals is about five times greater for people from the West Indies – greater than would be expected given their percentage of population (Rack, 1982). One social worker (Aros-Atolagbe, 1990) writes that second generation black people in the UK suffer tremendous crises of cultural identification; alienation produces more stress which may precipitate a temporary breakdown.

Although individual and ethnic-group variations exist, many immigrants similarly go through a pattern of adaptation to an unfamiliar, and probably discriminating, environment. The loss of support networks together with a sense of powerlessness means that the process of emigrating goes through critical phases such as:

excitement → disenchantment → perception of discrimination → identification crisis → and marginal acceptance

(see Hirayama and Cetingok, 1988 and Marris, 1986 who discuss the loss of one's homeland, which decidedly was my experience when I once emigrated).

The *signs of someone in crisis* actually might be difficult to spot, as we saw with Mrs Todd and Mr Smith. However, like grief, some of the responses follow a typical or classical pathway and this can give us some clues. We know that in the period of distress the person is striving to gain control and is open to suggestions which will aid recovery: phrases may include 'I can't cope', 'I feel a failure', 'I don't know where to turn' or 'It is hopeless'. (With Paula in the previous chapter's case example, she did not even know which words would express her crisis.) Often thoughts and behaviour are agitated, confused, hostile, ashamed or helpless. People may become irritable or withdrawn from their friends and relatives. Attempts to solve difficulties seem chaotic and unfocused. One client, unhappy in his new department at work, walked around all day muttering to himself; this could have been mistaken for a form of mental illness rather than the man's anxiety at losing his previous well-known routines. Other signs may be physiological, so that complaints about sleeplessness, tension and headaches (see Parry, 1990) may be mentioned by someone in crisis.

Techniques of crisis intervention

The techniques for intervening in crisis situations are sketched now which will help you in the initial, ongoing and final stages. In the first interview it is essential that the focus is kept on the present circumstances of the crisis event. Asking 'What happened?' thereby encourages the person's *cognitive grasp* of their situation. Comments such as 'You must feel awful' or 'No wonder you are upset' help to draw out the affective responses (i.e. feelings) which block thinking. The worker and client together try to make an assessment of the actual event and the causes which seem to have triggered it. It is necessary to gauge what ego strengths someone has so that their normal coping resources can be gleaned. The case of Paula in the previous chapter demonstrated how the worker took into account the woman's limited social skills when deciding how active resource mobilisation needed to be: questions which assist in this include: 'When did things start to go wrong?'; 'How did you try to handle this?'; 'What happened then?'; 'What is happening now?' and 'Which supports can you call on?'. (With Paula, drawing her network map revealed the possible support of an older sister.)

Having gained some idea of available and potential resources, the worker outlines the next step, asking 'What is the most pressing problem?' or 'What is bothering you most?'. The client is then asked to settle on one target area, the worker confirming this by saying 'So the most important thing is . . .?'. Obviously, these are not formulae for copying, they are suggestions as to what to cover in the initial period of disorganisation when the worker conveys hope, shows commitment to persevering while cutting the overwhelming problem down into manageable bits (known as partialising the problem). A contract for further work is spelled out in specific, concrete terms such as 'Let's concentrate on . . . You do . . . I'll do . . .'.Optimism is used to reduce the client's anxiety and perception of hopelessness: concreteness helps to keep the person in touch with reality. The aim at this early stage is to start to build a relationship based, not on time, but on the worker's expertise and authenticity, again to restore the client's sense of trust.

As the client's thinking is clarified, it is necessary to re-establish a sense of autonomy, by giving him/her something to do before the next meeting. This can be achieved, for instance with someone frozen into inaction, by getting them to say when next you need to meet again. In any event, letting individuals decide on the schedule for help such as 'I think I need to see you four more times over the next two weeks' builds self-reliance into the agreement and prevents undue dependence in the longer term.

Further contact in the middle phase sees the worker centring on obtaining missing data, for example, 'Can you tell me more about . . .?' The emphasis is still on the here-and-now but there may be links with past conflicts not recognised in the earlier phase of staying with the presenting issues. Pointing out possible connections helps the person to correct cognitive perception while keeping the problem, rather than fantasy or distortion, in the foreground. The helper has to be the voice of reality (Golan, 1978) showing the difference between 'what is' (real) and 'if only . . .'. Maybe the client Mr Smith would have wished he could have his 'whole' daughter back as if the accident had not happened; but that was not possible and plans had to be made to assist her and others to live with her disability.

Letting the person talk helps to relieve tension; ventilating feelings can release mental energy for tackling past worries. Help is given to sort out what worked and did not work in attempting to solve the problems; 'So you did . . . Did it work . . .?' Alternative solutions are weighed; exploring overlooked resources assists in restoring equilibrium and also develops a pattern (i.e. new habits) in being able to use such help in the future. By sorting out specific tasks together, aiming for achievable goals, the social worker acts as a role model for competent problem solving; for instance, setting homework, 'Before we next meet I'd like you to think how you could . . .', sets the stage for encouraging a change in thinking, feeling and action.

The termination phase of crisis intervention, perhaps the last two interviews, should have been built into the original agreement. Once the state of crisis is overcome and homeostasis restored, it would be harmful to prolong this type of approach as it could ignore natural growth potential present in all human beings. Reminding the client how much time there is left, reviewing progress and planning for the future prevent dependency (i.e. lowered functioning). However, premature termination, 'I can cope now, so I don't want to see you anymore', could be a 'flight into health' (Rapoport, 1970) not a well-thought-through decision. We shall explore endings in more detail in the final chapter.

Framework for understanding crisis intervention

A framework for understanding crisis intevention in summary form follows:

Theories and important concepts which contribute to the identification of crisis developed from:

(a) Psychoanalytic theories of personality (see Chapter 5) where the ego directs energy for problem solving, appraises reality and helps us to cope, adapt and master conflicts.
(b) Erikson (1965), building on ego psychology, suggests that we grow by managing psychosocial crisis points, which are transitional points in our life-cycle towards maturity.
(c) Learning theory contributes in relation to ideas about cognitive perception, role modelling and repetitive rehearsal of effective problem solving (see Chapter 6).
(d) These contributions fuse with those from research into grief reactions (Lindemann, 1965) and those of time-limited, task focused work dealt with in the following chapter.

Problems for which this approach is applicable may not even seem like problems. They can be changes such as becoming a teenager, as well as situational or unanticipated crises such as promotion or illness. Furthermore, as we have seen, crises can occur at any time when a person perceives a threat to their life goals. It is the meaning of the event to the unique individual which matters. Problems are usually current and pressing ones; routine early history taking would be inappropriate. So too would organizational arrangements such as waiting lists or long-drawn-out allocation procedures. Chronic crisis situations cannot be dealt with by this approach – longer term, in-depth work is often necessary.

Goals are kept to a minimum. They include relief of current life stressors, restoration to the previous level of coping, learning to understand what precipitated the condition, planning what the client can do to maintain maximum autonomy and contact with reality, and finding out what other resources could be used. When current stresses have their origins in past life experiences, the goal might be to help the person to come to terms with earlier losses to reduce the risk of future vulnerability.

The client's role is to review and question the hazardous event in order to understand how the state of crisis occurred. At times, clients take unwise decisions or make inappropriate suggestions for solving the problem so the worker takes advantage of the person's lowered defences and willingness to take advice, thereby inhibiting flight, e.g. premature plans for the future. Indeed, a lot of the work for the client is to remember that there *is* a future. By 'telling the story to themselves' cognitive awareness is improved. Sharing the experience and the feelings with family or others in the support network strengthens these resources which, in their distress, some clients forget are there. Disintegration is also prevented when the client assumes responsibility for some small practical task.

The worker's role is to give information and advice, to be active, directive and systematic, if need be. It is essential to be authentic as part of the promotion of reality testing and adjustment. Setting time limits, for example four to six contacts, encourages the person to face up to the future without fear or shame that they will never be independent again. While cognitive restructuring and release of tension are the aims of this approach, self-understanding need not be part of the worker's plan for the client; rather, teaching how to split problems into manageable pieces and acting as a role model for effective problem solving in the acute stage is what is required. To do this, the social worker must put themselves into a position of 'standing still', i.e. remaining calm and being able to 'bear it' when confronted with someone in crisis. The danger in crisis intervention is that the caregivers, surrounded by people who want something done, usually a 'plea to remove someone' (O'Hagan, 1986), will almost go into crisis themselves, not thinking clearly about what needs to be done. (You will remember with the case example of Paula in Chapter 2 that neighbours and the police reacted by asking the social worker to remove the children. The worker did not respond to their panic and kept calm.)

Prior to introducing the literature on coping with catastrophe, which is related to crisis concepts, I want to briefly comment on *preventive work*. Over the years it seems to have been a neglected aspect of crisis intervention; if there are two types of crisis, those which can be foreseen such as life-cycle transitions and those which are accidental or unforeseen such as sudden bereavement then there is scope in the former to prepare for the change. Because maturational crises can be anticipated, public health systems which operate services to maintain mental health could be developed further. Of course, politically, any preventive service is likely to be threatened when there are cutbacks. But it is somewhat short-sighted of social policy planners and social services to simply react to crises on a case-by-case basis. And yet, when economies are made they frequently hit hardest at agencies which actively deal with health education, pre-school experiences, ante-natal support, preparation for retirement, drugs information bureaux, marriage guidance counselling and schemes for preparation/consultation when large-scale rehousing schemes are planned. Moreover, even with tragedies, considered in a moment, many of these are actually 'man-made', such as wars, traffic accidents and toxic waste disasters – here too, preventive action, known as *primary prevention* is possible with co-ordinated services made ready to prevent long-term psychological and other effects. We know that on an individual level, 'anticipatory worry work' helps later grieving, as do ceremonial rituals practised for a long time after a death by some cultures (Raphael, 1984; Parkes, 1986): so why are our services not geared to lowering the incidence of mental disorder?

Crisis intervention at a *secondary preventive level*, that is help geared to people who are in crisis, equally is at risk from unenlightened policy makers. For instance, funding threats continually face organisations such as women's refuges, rape crisis services, suicide prevention centres, and substance abuse rehabilitation units. As we have seen, help given at the right time, when a person is psychologically amenable, can prevent long-term use of any of these systems. Fortunately, some recognition of how we can set up *tertiary prevention* services (the help given to those people who have actually been made worse by earlier intervention), can be seen in the efforts to re-establish long-term patients from psychiatric hospitals back in the community. If community care does become established then truly we could begin to practise primary, preventive crisis intervention, not simply by putting right harmful interventions but by interfering with destructive forces affecting health.

Coping with catastrophe

Only now is the literature related to managing severe trauma and co-ordinating all the support services for major incidents beginning to appear (Raphael, 1986; Hodgkinson and Stewart, 1991). While the horrors of kidnaps, famine, floods, fires, epidemics, mass murder, transport and technology accidents are not new, high standards of safety may have been traded for cost-cutting making these events more likely? In any case, certainly in many welfare departments, emergency strategy meetings used to occur only occasionally. Now with the eclipsing events of war, large personal social service organisations have to ensure that they constantly monitor their disaster plans, learning from tragedies such as Hillsborough, Lockerbie and Piper Alpha. These incidents have revealed the long-term psychological effects of trauma and how early counselling of survivors, bereaved relatives and friends and those in the rescue services can prevent pathological outcomes in the years which follow.

While the definitions of disaster imply extraordinary seriousness and great human suffering, there are many overlapping characteristics of relevance to both crisis and catastrophe: both are marked by rapid time sequences, disruption of usual coping responses, perceptions of threat and helplessness, major changes in behaviour and a turning to others for help (Raphael, 1986). Similarly, personal tragedies such as the loss of a loved one by violent means or someone who has been diagnosed to have AIDS will produce reactions such as shock, disbelief, denial, magical thinking, depersonalisation, sleep disorders, depression, anger, guilt and isolation. Sudden death or losses of any kind produce syndromes characteristic of disaster responses. Thus, a colleague whose father had been murdered endured a complicated and prolonged bereavement process.

The time phases of disaster i.e.:

threat → impact → taking stock of the effects → rescue and recovery

resemble those of crisis reactions, though there tends to be post-disaster euphoria at having survived and immediate convergence from far and wide to help the stricken community. Nevertheless, the predominant need for people in states of crisis and those affected by disaster is for *information* by which to make meaning of such overpowering experiences, seeking to understand by describing what happened, and trying to restore some sense of mastery over the powerlessness which the very thought of extraordinary destruction brings.

So, even though many practitioners may never encounter catastrophes, they are of interest to any agency who is interested in providing sensitive, compassionate treatment and drawing up preventive programmes alongside those which manage psychosocial care in the aftermath. (One of the reasons that we know so much about the dimensions of grief is due partly to people like Lindemann, quoted above, who studied the survivors of a night-club fire.) Raphael (1986) suggests that we should study these phenomena because:

- They give an insight into the common responses of individuals and groups, revealing universal themes of survival, loss and long-term adaptation.
- Prediction and counterdisaster activities together with guidelines for co-ordinating help can be drawn up.
- Knowledge can be applied to individual, everyday disasters, stress and life events.

When setting up post-disaster aftercare those involved in counselling the survivors need to assess and understand background variables related to the nature of the community which has suffered the impact. Their patterns of communication and access to it; their view towards the authorities and agencies which give direction; cultural and ethnic issues; how dependent/independent and urban/rural the community is; how integrated/loose-knit are networks; the interpretations made of the disaster; any special individuals whose qualities could influence responses are some of the factors to be taken into account. An overview of welfare systems is required as is epidemiological data such as mortality and morbidity rates so that public health planning and co-ordination of the relief services such as police and ambulance is effective.

There are many different ways in which people attempt to gain mastery in the immediate post-disaster phase. These can include *talking through*, putting into words (and therefore outside oneself), the meaning of the experience. On the other hand, someone who tells their story again and again with no emotional abreaction can become locked into the experience. *Giving testimony*, wanting to write about or talk on the media about the process is a further attempt to gain control over the events and to guide others in the future.

Feelings are often the most difficult to release, perhaps only coming later when the catastrophe is safely behind. Long after impact sensory perceptions may remain as frightening memories. For instance, the awful noise accompanying any event or the terrible silence and stillness; vivid visual experiences and the smell of the disaster haunted those who survived the Bradford fire. *Tears* are important in the release of feelings, maybe triggered by others' grief and distress, though difficult for some men or cultures where they are viewed as weakness. Caregivers, such as ambulance personnel, doctors or social workers are sometimes hidden victims of disasters when they are assumed to be invulnerable. Communal rituals and public acknowledgement of suffering may also help tears and anger but generally feelings have to come out bit by bit when the person can gradually test out how they feel. *Perception of the future* and the need to get on with the demands of living is a signal that recovery has started; some trust in the world and hope returns; certain survivors become more aware of what matters to them and have a greater insight into their coping resources (see Raphael, 1986).

Raphael (1986) reveals studies into how children and elderly people cope and shows that both are more resilient than we might imagine. False protection from truths, such as not attending a funeral or being given inconsistent answers to questions (see, for instance, Black, 1979), may put children's coping at risk. Repetitive re-enactment play has been found to lessen fear and helplessness – when I worked in Australia, children whose community had been hit by a tornado, built a large dragon monster which they all 'attacked': drawings and writing too can facilitate mastery.

As mentioned earlier, care for workers and helpers is an important component of any treatment approaches. Psychological debriefing to lessen the stress of encounters with death and devastation prevents illness which can arise out of feelings of depression at not being able to do more. Or lack of preparation for the role, whether through lack of training or shock, may require support. Many of the helpers in the Liverpool/Hillsborough teams found that they had to re-learn counselling skills so that they could empathise with large numbers of people unloading all their grief and anger upon them. Support groups are useful, especially because they do not make the helpers feel that they have failed or that they are themselves somehow being psychoanalysed. Group processes, as we shall see in Chapter 8, help members to explore their reactions, reviewing positive and negative aspects in order to integrate (that is, be able to look at a distance and retrospectively), at what was learned for one-self, for others and for the future.

Case example

Tom, aged thirty-two and living at home with his family, was referred to a specialist service dealing with post-traumatic stress disorders. He had served some years before in the Falklands war where massive confrontation with the deaths of others and disfiguring injuries had not been integrated: these kinds of experiences do not easily go away and do not fade readily from mind. Tom felt that he had encountered hell on earth. Stressors such as words or places (such as Sheffield), brought back all the intensity of the violence; he had recurrent dreams of the events, was hyperalert and gradually became irritable and aggressive with his family.

When he had first returned home everyone was elated that he had survived. He too was only too glad to join in the celebration and forget what he had gone through; after several weeks his family expected him to get on with living and to 'put it all behind him'. Unfortunately, Tom could not do this: he had endured terrible smells, sounds and seen the mutilation of others; encountering violent death for the first time in his life he was preoccupied with death and the war, which after a time, no one wanted to listen to. He buried the intrusive images of his experiences and tried to get on with his life.

What was worse, Tom had actually shut out the fact that he had been exposed to the killing of his closest comrade. Both had been under fire when his friend was killed at his side. Tom had carried on in the battle as if it had never happened. So effective was his denial that he joined with the other soldiers to rejoice when the battle was won; this psychic numbness helped him through, protecting him from what is dreadful about war – that killing may be necessary for personal survival. It stopped him feeling, not only then, but for some years. As some Vietnam veterans complained, 'I can't feel for people like I used to'. Thus, on discharge, he continued to protect his ego, his defence against death anxiety and guilt. His family became tired of his inability to 'pull himself together' and, believing that 'the Falklands' were a thing of the past, did not want to listen to his accounts. He therefore became isolated, depressed and withdrawn and was referred to mental health workers skilled in treating post-traumatic stress disorder.

Usually, treatment methods include individual, family and group approaches, using behavioural techniques and counselling. The client was helped in abreactive sessions to try to remember the blur of events on the day that his friend was killed. In groups, other survivors and he drew their anger and their pain in order to externalise their feelings. After some weeks, Tom was helped to face the detail of what had happened on the day of loss, what he had been doing and so on in detail.

A breakthrough occurred when he at last was able to shed tears for the first time. Like other people who want to give testimony to what the experience meant and how others may gain from it, Tom wrote about his recovery. His account begins:

> I think now that at last the war is over for me, though it will always be there for me for the rest of my days. Looking back, I have come to realize that we fight our battles on two fronts; one against the enemy in our sights, the other against the enemy within ourselves.

4

Task-centred Practice

In the 1950s Helen Harris Perlman attempted to give unity to practice by focusing on it as a problem-solving process (Perlman, 1957): as we saw in the previous chapter, choosing and accomplishing tasks is an essential part of human coping endeavours. In this chapter, I show how this emphasis on substantive factors and concrete problems was developed into a well-specified set of procedures called the task-centred approach. Some of the research into its effectiveness will highlight the main ideas. How it differs from crisis intervention will be briefly explored. Again I offer a framework for understanding, summarising the components of task-centred work, while case examples illustrate the methods in action.

How the task-centred approach developed

It seems hard to believe, in this era of short-term work, contracts with clients and setting up evaluations of projects, that for many years between 1920 and the 1960s practitioners tended to concentrate less on problem-solving processes and more on in-depth assessment and the client–worker relationship. Models of practice therefore tended to involve long-term work, exploration of clients' feelings, a tendency to talk about, rather than take action on difficulties and an interest in underlying, rather than presenting problems. Consequently, some clients received help for years and compulsive care-giving by helpers often resulted in the difficulties becoming the responsibility and 'property' of the worker (Buckle, 1981).

I remember that in my early days as a mental welfare officer I kept cases open for years: visiting was done on a friendly but aimless basis; providing pre-care or after-care services was the global aim but there were few specific goals to accomplish, with or without the clients' agreement. I suppose I was what Davies (1985) calls a 'maintenance mechanic': he says this is a key social work role and suggests that craving for change is textbook idealism. However, proponents of task-centred practice would disagree. They would propose that social work should be a focused activity and, owing a debt to Perlman (1957), should educate clients to become good at problem solving. Furthermore, with today's emphasis on efficiency, effectiveness and economy, we are having to justify our services and prove to those who fund us that social work works. This is not an easy statement to prove (although the quasi-experimental work done in Kent and Gateshead by Challis and his team (see Challis and Davies, 1989; Davies and Knapp, 1988) actually proved that change was possible with frail elderly people, whose quality of life improved with goal-directed resources aimed at keeping them where they chose to be – in their own homes.)

So, how did we reach this position of being able to show the relationship between inputs and outcomes? In North America, in 1969, a four-year study into brief versus extended casework was published (Reid and Shyne, 1969). Clients in a large voluntary agency dealing with family welfare were offered two contrasting 'packages' of social work intervention: one was an experimental brief service of Planned Short-Term Treatment (PSTT), consisting of eight interviews; the other was the usual practice in the agency of long-term service lasting up to eighteen months. To everyone's surprise, the clients in the short-term group improved more than those given the continued service. In fact the latter tended to deteriorate! The authors hypothesised that a law of diminishing returns was operating. Once help is extended beyond a certain point, clients may lose confidence in their own ability to cope (as intimated in crisis intervention) and become dependent on the worker or the agency with whom they may develop a kind of negative attachment.

In addition, when improvement or change does occur, the study revealed that this is likely to occur early on in 'treatment', regardless of the worker's implicit long-term goals.

This research was taken up in Britain by researchers at the National Institute for Social Work and elsewhere in the 1970s and 1980s, which we shall come to in a moment. The vital elements in the initial Reid and Shyne experiment appeared to be that *brief periods of service, concentrating on limited goals chosen by the client*, were often more effective and more durable than open-ended work. It seemed that setting a time limit led to the expectation that rapid change would occur, thus increasing the motivation and energy of all the participants. The North American projects in the 1960s concentrated on advice giving and active exploration of problems. They aimed for unambitious, specified goals. Moreover, their performance was committed and hopeful (these might have been placebo effects, adding to the success. But, in any case, consumer satisfaction studies always mention worker qualities as important (Sainsbury, 1986)).

The first book describing 'task-centred practice' as such appeared in 1972 (Reid and Epstein) giving the results of the tests into the elements of the approach which seemed to be linked to its success. By that time, an even more systematic and goal-directed framework had been produced which suggested that there should be a maximum of twelve interviews within three months, again focusing on limited, achievable goals which are chosen by the client. From then on, social workers who tried out the idea were instrumental in helping to further refine the model (Reid and Epstein, 1977).

Currently, task-centred practice deals with *eight problem areas* (which cover most of the referrals met with by practitioners). They are:

Interpersonal conflict
Dissatisfaction in social relations
Problems with formal organisations

Difficulties in role performance
Problems of social transition
Reactive emotional distress
Inadequate resources
Behavioural problems (Reid, 1978; Reid and Hanrahan, 1981).

There are definite steps to be taken in the process of problem solving, i.e. *five phases* in helping clients to achieve their own modest goals.

1. *Problem exploration* when clients' concerns are elicited, clarified, defined in explicit, behavioural terms and ranked in order of importance to the client.
2. *Agreement* is reached with the client on the target for change, which is then classified by the worker under the previous eight categories.
3. *Formulating an objective* which has been decided jointly. Agreement is reached on the frequency and duration of the contract. (In respect of contracts which are written, it is as well to clarify the traditions of certain social classes and minority ethnic groups, as the 'legal' concept may be misunderstood. Of course, such contracts in social work are not legally binding but simply clarify respective tasks and roles.)
4. *Achieving the task(s)*, for which no prescribed methods or techniques are proposed within task-centred literature.
5. *Termination* is built in from the beginning. When reviewing the achievements, the worker's efforts are examined, not merely those of the client or the other helping networks.

Throughout the development of this approach in North America, parallel research was being conducted in the UK by Matilda Goldberg and her colleagues (Goldberg *et al.*, 1977). They found that the model, used by a social service department area team in Buckinghamshire applied to only a minority of clients, at least in its 'pure' form. Those with a need for practical resources who acknowledged that they had a problem fared best. Involuntary/unwilling clients or those who had chronic, complex problems were less amenable. Having said this, there were positive gains for the workers in the project who improved their capacity for clearer thinking and forward planning. Tackling small, manageable objectives, rather than vague global ones, proved more realistic. (For example, one of my students ought not to have been surprised recently when a fourteen-year-old boy on a supervision order re-offended, despite having a contract to behave himself: the contract stated that the goal would be to stop offending; not only is this a negative way of putting things (doing something positive is preferred), but the objective was too ambitious and stated in 'world-wide' terms. Far better to aim low, for instance, a weekly contract that he will visit his 'gran' and try to keep out of trouble (e.g. not steal cars).) Also, social workers in the project found themselves less guilty about being unable to sort out everything, the Utopian cure-all which we all foolishly try to cope with.

Subsequently, Goldberg's team set up three experimental projects using task-centred work in a probation department, in two intake teams and in a hospital social work department (Goldberg *et al.*, 1985). As the findings and conclusions hold for all three settings and client groups they are worth summarising, plus they give us an up-to-date and rounded picture of where this model presently stands. Task-centred methods proved applicable to between a half and two thirds of all cases. The remaining groups largely ended the attempt to be task-centred after the problem search (phase 1) resulted in no agreement about the target problem. On the other hand, most clients who completed all five phases were pleased with the approach and said that their problems were reduced. The clients who could not be helped included those we looked at in the last chapter whose life style centred around chronic 'cliff-hanging' episodes and those whose difficulties were deep-seated and longer term.

The skills required of the workers included an ability to listen and grasp what the client was truly bothered about; to know when to use systematic communication styles and when to be responsive (this is analysed below); to have the ability to renegotiate the contract or agreement; to act as an empowering partner, not just a service provider; to be explicit about time limits, and to remind the client about ending the contact, without harping on this. Difficulties were encountered by social workers who recognised that it was not authentic to treat clients as equals when they have no control over resources or when people were under surveillance as part of statutory duties such as a probation order.

To take the last point a little further: while the task-centred approach and the notion of empowerment might be to move towards 'power-to-the-people', ultimately, as we can see from the sphere of practice in welfare bureaucracies, we lean towards accountability towards other professionals rather than towards consumers. In addition, where there are perceived risks, agencies are loth to adopt time limits. Of course, client self-determination and respect for persons are the accepted values of our profession (though hotly debated in the *British Journal of Social Work*, see Webb and McBeath, 1990). There nevertheless remain possibilities inherent in task-centred work of changing from service provision to service brokerage as community care plans show (Department of Health, 1989). In the process of developing this approach in the future, perhaps we can seek ways in which the client's independence and opportunities for choice may be promoted. Certainly, the accounts of creative problem-solving with elderly people (Challis *et al.,* 1990) would indicate that, within the processes of case management, is the seed for the growth of this method of practice.

Returning to the point about having to acquire the technique of simultaneously using two styles of communicating: it is specified in Reid and Epstein (1972) that communication be systematic and responsive, that is, keeping the client to the agreed task in hand, so as to reach the target problem and remaining empathic to the client's messages, respecting their value. On occasion, this feels to be something of a paradoxical expectation. The worker's responses should ensure that the client's problem solving does not become diffuse, but clients have a tendency to wander from the point, discussing matters which are not part of the agreed focus. If, for instance, I have a client who has a chosen objective to control their children's behaviour and each time we meet the discussion wanders on to marital circumstances, I would be in a quandary. Is communication becoming unsystematic or is the marital disharmony a more important problem? Or is it connected to the children's behaviour and therefore a central feature? There is always a possibility that the orginal problem search and agreed target problems are no longer valid, that goals will have to be redefined. Of course, in practice, it is permissible to allow for some wider discussion and then, in view of the limited time available, to bring the client back to the task. Alternatively, it would be robot-like and unresponsive to cling to the contract and it might be necessary to say, 'We often seem to get around to talking about your marriage. Do you think we should look again at what we've decided to do?'. Of itself responsiveness will not bring about change; structuring the work may. Ensuring that we have really understood what a problem means to someone requires, as we have seen in earlier chapters, giving attention to the client's communications and not introducing ideas which are only of interest to the worker. Combining this with a structured use of time and planned strategies helps to accomplish change in a step-by-step fashion.

   To give some idea how you can preserve both qualities, of systematic and responsive communications; you may convey that you understand that there are many other difficulties but that a start has to be made somewhere if the person does not want to become overwhelmed; an explanation could be given at the beginning of the process that each area selected by the client will eventually be discussed in detail. The point is to remain flexible; sometimes a passing remark seemingly unconnected to the task focus might be worth looking into rather than let it pass or change the subject. Thus, a woman who is worrying about her rent arrears may hint that her partner gets out of control when disciplining her children. Or, a client might say, 'I'm confused'. Such an incomplete sentence could hide many meanings which are worth bringing to the surface by asking, 'About what?'; once, when I was interviewing a young mother about her inability to feel anything for her baby, she

said, 'Nobody cares'. By enquiring who specifically does not
care about what, she revealed her perception of having been
rejected by her own mother. It is always useful to spot when
clients and others delete, distort or generalise their experiences using words such as nobody, never, always and so on.

The benefits of using task-centred methods

Before I go on to discuss when task-centred practice might
be used and how the approach compares with crisis intervention, I wish to summarise the main benefits as I may have
sounded a little negative about it until now. First, and most
importantly, task-centred does not mean simply assigning
tasks, or setting 'homework' such as is common in behavioural and family therapies. It is a well-researched, feasible,
and cost-effective method of working, which consumer
feedback indicates is very helpful to the majority of parties
(Butler *et al.*, 1978; Gibbons *et al.*, 1979). It offers a specific
set of procedures where clients are helped to carry out
problem-alleviating tasks within agreed periods of time. For
me, the client is the main change agent, helping the worker
to assess and choose what the priorities for change ought to
be (even if we have other ideas) and then agreeing who is
going to do what.

Task-centred practice fits well into intake teams (Buckle,
1981) which appear to be losing favour in many social service
offices which have become specialised or decentralised; yet
most still retain some kind of duty system and short-term
projects. A large number of the interdisciplinary teams set
up to establish community care for those with learning
disabilities and mental illness use a form of task-centred
practice, basing their goals on what is worked out with
service users, in addition to having a pre-planned exit time.
Currently one team I know are working with a sixty-two-
year-old, capable woman who spent over fifty years in a
mental hospital; they have allocated three months of their
budget to assisting her to learn how to use a bus route and to
settle in with her companions in a group care sheltered
housing scheme. A further task-centred set of goals will be

worked out with her, if she wishes, once these early practical tasks are achieved.

Any practice which ensures that there is no misunderstanding about why contact is taking place is likely to be more successful – if only because it is more honest and does not build up false expectations. It also means that where the social worker is acting as an agent of social control or is intent upon offering protection that there is no ambiguity about this. The use of task-centred ideas is welcomed also by black practitioners (Devore and Schlesinger, 1981) and by Solomon's (1976) black empowerment strategies, since the methods do not further oppress people by taking over their lives or implying that the worker knows best. There is no mystery about what the worker is doing because she/he is as accountable as the client in carrying out agreed tasks. This lessens the sense of powerlessness when faced with 'authority' figures.

Apart from the somewhat rigid time limits, which possibly ignore certain ethnic traditions which prefer slow entry into family and community relations, task-centred work is beneficial in that it:

1. Takes into account not only individual but also collective experiences during the stages of problem search, agreement and setting tasks. The source of the problem is not presumed to reside 'in' the client; as much attention is paid to external factors, such as welfare rights and housing, where there is scope for supplying 'power' resources such as information and knowledge (Hirayama and Cetingok, 1988). The role for the worker is one of resource consultant.
2. Like other approaches, such as the Psychosocial and Behavioural in Chapters 5 and 6, the focus can be on individuals, couples, families, groups and organisations. Practical advice on how to approach problems and systems can be rehearsed, modified and copied in groups; peers, as well as social workers, can act as teacher/ trainers in problem solving (Northen, 1982).
3. Addresses the strengths of people and their networks. For instance, it is an antidote to assuming being black is a

problem; there is scope to use the resources of black communities (Ahmad, 1990). One aim of the method is to enhance self-esteem as well as problem solving.
4. Does not rely on the notion of self-disclosure via a one-way, vertical helping relationship; it tries to put worker and client on the same footing.

Despite not always going as smoothly as the later case examples suggest, I particularly like the over-arching usefulness of this approach; it does not require a search for 'suitable referrals' as even those which look as though they will not 'fit' may benefit from *task-centred assessments*. Here, the first two phases of problem exploration and classification can help everyone to see things more clearly and know what the work will entail. Similarly, some clients find it difficult to actually pinpoint the source of their distress or difficulty and again a partially task-centred approach could offer clearer definition, from whence they may choose not to go ahead or to be helped using an alternative method such as those found elsewhere in this book. I mentioned earlier that it could be useful too in working with organisations; if you examine the management technology called Management by Objectives (MBO) you will see that it resembles task-centred practice, having agreed goals within a time-limited perspective (Coulshed, 1990): in relation to staff and student supervision, also, some practitioners find it valuable having agreed set tasks and in-built mechanisms for mutual evaluation.

Lastly, we should not overlook the use of time itself as a therapeutic agent; working within a time limit pushes forward the process. As one client expressed it, 'A good idea, can't depend on someone all my life' (Butler *et al.*, 1978, p. 407).

Comparison with crisis intervention

What are the differences between this approach and that of crisis intervention? While both encompass brief, focal work and may be used when clients are temporarily unable to sort out their own problems and are better able to then use help to improve coping in a time-limited framework, I must point out that, in my view, this is as far as the similarity goes. Some of the research into the effectiveness of task-centred practice seems to have been tried with people who were in a state of crisis. We recognised in the previous chapter that people often then cannot 'think straight', they cannot easily conceptualise their problems or the solutions without fairly heavy dependency on the worker in the initial and mid-way stages. Certainly, those in crisis are not ready for an energetic, problem-solving, equitable relationship with a worker, able to agree to a detailed contract which needs to be carefully thought through and planned. It may be that both methods handle significant social, emotional and practical difficulties – but these need not be crises in the accepted sense. We know that, even with some flexibility, the work under discussion in this chapter tends to be systematic, focusing on one task at a time; goals are behaviourally specified, the whole programme tightly scheduled to fit a maximum of twelve to fourteen interviews, the ending predetermined rather than dependent on the psychological recovery of the person in crisis. Turbulent change can occur in crises which call for worker responsiveness which is not necessarily goal directed. In sum, clients in crisis are unlikely to be able to cope with the demands of a fully-task-centred approach.

Some techniques in each of the five phases

Once again, these are not recipes for action; merely some notion of what is likely to crop up in the sequence of phases towards problem resolution.

In the *initial contact, exploration and agreement phases* (say between one and six contacts), if the client is not self-referred:

– find out what the referrer's goals are
– negotiate specific goals and if these can be time-limited
– negotiate with the referrer what resources they will offer to achieve these goals.

If the client applies independently and voluntarily:

- encourage the client to articulate their problems
- encourage ventilation of feelings about these
- step in with immediate practical help if necessary
- assist the person to take some action on their own, something small and achievable
- elicit the array of problems with which the client is currently concerned
- explain how the task-centred approach works, e.g. time limits; priority focus; schedule for interviews; anyone else who needs to be involved, such as family member
- define the stated problems in specific, behavioural terms
- tentatively determine target problems with client
- choose a maximum of three problems ranked for priority by the client
- classify the problems under the eight categories
- list the problems in a contract, if used

Formulating objectives and achieving the tasks (say between the fourth and tenth contact):

- make the task selection phase short; if the targeting of problems has been done carefully, this will indicate what/ who needs to change
- get the client to think out her/his own tasks and what effects will be likely, helping if the client's assessment looks unrealistic, will make things worse or can not be achieved in the time
- if other people are involved, get their agreement too
- if need be, help the client to generate alternatives and identify what resources are around
- support task performance by a variety of problem-solving means. For instance: refer to a specialised source if this is required (e.g. debt counselling, vocational guidance, classes to learn a language); demonstrate or use games/ stimulations/video; rehearse problem solving; report back how it went; accompany client for moral support; discuss client's fears, plans, resources; regularly record the status of the problem; examine obstacles and failures in detail
- if other areas of concern emerge, decide in collaboration with the client if these are worth pursuing

- always ask about all the tasks in case failures are not
  mentioned
- if the method has been modified as partially task-centred
  (e.g. for assessment only or time limits are not part of the
  contract) consider what follow-up or alternatives will be
  used

Termination (hard to predict how long the process takes in
each situation but say the final two to three contacts):

- talk about what will be the effect of ending the contact
- find ways of helping clients to cope with anxieties
- review progress and give encouragement
- help clients to identify further areas of work
- extend time limits only if clients feel that they need extra
  time and have shown commitment to working on tasks
- monitor only when mandated by agency or legal requirements or if part of a community care 'package'
- evaluate each person's inputs and record outcomes
- say goodbye sensitively.

For further information on task-centred processes, Epstein
(1980) offers a detailed map of the model in action.

Case examples

Mr Taylor was a fifty-seven-year-old widower who had spent
his working life as a ship's captain. Travelling around the
world had left him with no friends in his locality and his
married son, who lived many miles away, could only visit
him two or three times a year. Following a stroke six months
previously the client had 'vegetated' in a facility for disabled
people. Rehabilitation efforts had ceased: staff complained
that Mr Taylor was uncooperative and aggressive; they even
wondered if he was clinically depressed, as he slumped all
day in a wheelchair, keeping himself to himself.

The social worker received a referral from the care staff to
sort out the numerous debts which had accrued because the
client had not claimed any benefits. She found that Mr
Taylor, far from being hostile, was a gentle, shy man who
was not used to discussing his private affairs. When he heard

about the task-centred ideas, which would not pry into his background, he was pleased to talk about his problems. He defined these as 'problems with formal organisations' and 'inadequate resources'. The contract was agreed that they would meet weekly to work on two target problems:

1. To pay off rent, telephone and fuel bills within the following three months.
2. To claim outstanding benefits from social security, insurance companies and salary from previous employers.

General tasks, such as writing letters, listing the debts, making phone calls and deciding who would do what were dealt with in the first two meetings. A schedule was drawn up about the frequency and duration of the meetings (mornings and for twenty-five minutes as Mr Taylor tired easily). They agreed also to let the centre staff know what would happen.

Every Monday at the same time the social worker wheeled Mr Taylor to a pleasant spot where they discussed how the debts could be cleared and which were the most pressing.

Responsibilities were allocated and each week they reviewed each other's task accomplishments. Sometimes the worker had to obtain necessary forms and give the client instructions on how to complete them, but no revision of the contract was needed. The client not only cleared his debts and claimed his allowances, but also began to talk about his past life as a ship's captain and to discuss how he might manage in the future.

Mr Taylor, in one of these discussions, confided to the worker his fear of returning home to live alone, and his loneliness at not knowing any neighbours. He talked about his shyness which had even stopped him getting to know anyone in the unit. Accepting that he had overcome his shyness with the worker, they examined ways in which to start a conversation, re-negotiating a further task-centred working agreement that:

1. He would start a conversation with one of his companions at lunch every day.

2. He would write to his son telling him how he had sorted
   out his finances, and ask if he would visit him some time.

Because the client's manner was so approachable, physio-
therapy and occupational therapy were restarted, resulting
in an ability to walk with a tripod. The son made a visit and
offered his father a home. The unit's carers marvelled at the
change, and, if there had been a multidisciplinary team
approach, all could have congratulated Mr Taylor for his
own efforts.

The second situation was met with by a student on a four
month community work placement. He was asked to make
an assessment of the needs felt by the residents in one street
which had achieved notoriety due to their 'criminal and
irresponsible' behaviour. Intervention by police, social services, social security and housing officials seemed to have
exacerbated the stigmatising and labelling of the tenants.
Their council houses were almost derelict: empty homes all
around were, in fact, devoid of roofs and floorboards
(stolen, it was alleged, by the deviant street dwellers).

Having completed a community profile (for ways of going
about this see the resource paper by Brewster, 1988) the
student started to make contact with the residents asking
them what they would like to see changed in the street.
Perhaps not surprisingly, the majority of people wanted the
professionals 'off their backs'; there were complaints about
being viewed as undesirables, even though most tenants
were coping with poverty and unemployment and yet still
had time to help one another. They disliked the housing
policy of putting temporary tenants in the empty houses,
giving the whole place a temporary feel and a bad name.
Although many in the street found it depressing, being
rehoused was not on their list of priorities. They liked their
close-knit networks.

The student found that one tenant had several daughters
and their children living in the street; this woman had been
an asset when a former community worker had tried to set
up summer play schemes. She told the student that most
people were angry with the Housing Department who
treated them as second-class citizens (whenever a temporary

resident moved on the council workmen rushed to board-up the property as if to deter the street's 'criminal' element from stealing anything). As spokesperson, she believed that the major goal was to have a meeting with housing officials and confront them with these dissatisfactions.

Although this was not a fully task-centred project, in that the student did not have the time to list all the other problems found in the survey and the overstretched full-time community worker could not have carried on the work, the main objective, of having a meeting with a person of authority from the Housing Department did take place. It was a well-planned meeting, in the home of the above tenant, and attended by other residents in the street. Their concerns were heard sympathetically. Now, some years later, the area has been refurbished as part of a larger, long-term initiative between the public and private sectors.

It might have been useful, as with all task-centred programmes, to have explained to the network of other agencies involved how goal-oriented, short-term, client-directed methods work. As it is, many systems (sometimes even our own), believe that social work will go on for ever. Comprehensive community care services in the future, involving health, social services, housing, voluntary and independent organisations, working together, might thereby halt any fairy-tale syndrome; planning in partnership might target care in a more systematic sense, especially when those who act as case managers are aware of task-centred ideas.

Framework for understanding task-centred practice

To conclude this chapter, a framework for understanding task-centred practice is shown below:

Theories which underly the task-centred approach are really only concepts: they include the crisis notion that focused help given at the right time is as effective as long-term service. Also, task accomplishment is viewed as an essential process in human coping endeavours, the choice of tasks and success in tackling them motivating people towards improved problem solving. Mastery of situations strengthens the ego, while success breeds success. Though no specific problem-oriented theory exists at this point, nevertheless the underlying values which guide this approach are that workers should state what they are trying to achieve and clients' self-esteem and independence is preserved when they are seen as experts of their own lives. The use of time limits conveys the message that change is possible in the time agreed and working to deadlines sometimes inspires commitment.

Problems are psychosocial in nature and comprise eight categories which describe problem situations rather than client types.

Goals are modest, achievable, specific and often framed in behavioural terms; they are chosen by the client in collaboration with the worker. Goals are inherent in each of the five phases, completion of which would qualify the approach as fully task-centred. However, a partially task-centred approach is possible when only some of these phases are reached: an example of this would be task-centred assessment.

The client's role is to identify desirable and feasible goals and to specify tasks and sub-tasks, prioritised in a working agreement with the social worker.

The worker's role is to make explicit the time limits to the client and the agencies involved and to assist in the problem search, target and task-setting by which problems are reduced and some solutions found.

Techniques are really activities, examples of which are:

(a) *Problem specification*, e.g. 'When you try to get your son to go to school, what does he do; who helps you; how do you react; what happens then?' etc.

(b) *Task planning* which incorporates agreeing tasks, planning detailed implementation, generating alternative solutions and summarising, e.g. 'So what else could you try; could you do this before we meet next time; will you ask your husband to back you up; are we clear about what we've agreed?' etc.

(c) *Analysing obstacles and failures* such as 'It sounds as though your husband says nothing when you try to get your son to go to school. What could we do to get him to help you more?'
(d) *Planning tasks*, the detail of 'Who will do what?'
(e) *Structuring interview time*, asking 'How long do you think we need?' and 'Our time is coming to an end, we have agreed . . .'
(f) *Reviewing and ending*, e.g. 'What did you think of the time limits; did they help or not in what you achieved?'

5

The Psychosocial Approach

We arrive now at the point where we can start to fill the gaps and answer some of the questions left by the earlier methods of practice. It may have struck you that there are situations which are difficult to change as well as people whose behaviour leaves even experienced workers puzzled and floundering. Then, assessment and intervention usually cannot be brief and straightforward. Methods of helping clients who wish to be freer from their emotional problems have to be found: some like to understand themselves and why they feel powerless to change. There are other clients for whom self-knowledge could be damaging or where such insight would seem to make no difference.

What can we offer people who show 'neurotic' tendencies; who cannot give 'good-enough' parenting; seem to be insatiably dependent on others; block out their emotions; 'act out' rather than talk through their difficulties, albeit that these are usually underlying rather than presenting problems? Such referrals are common to social work caseloads and are often the most demanding in terms of time, patience, practice wisdom and worker maturity. One treatment approach which provides a longer term, sustaining and nurturing relationship, at the same time as reducing external stress is the psychosocial approach, which this chapter considers.

The psychosocial approach as a method of understanding

Everyone, and that includes us, has vulnerabilities; we, like clients, sometimes do not know why certain events upset us or remind us of a part of the past which we would rather forget. As part of our duties, too, we could unconsciously slip into favouring one client group, e.g. children or women, over others, thereby risking the neglect of less 'attractive' clients on our workloads. This is why the worker needs to attempt self-understanding and why, moreover, there is a need to try to understand others so that we may accurately understand the *person as well as the problem*. If we accept and are to take into account that people have inner worlds and outer realities, then we have to understand the 'person-in-situation' whole (the psycho-social). Practice which automatically accepts that the presenting problem *is* the problem is likely to keep missing the point: I once ineffectively spent two years helping a woman with a rehousing problem, becoming intolerant when numerous house moves produced no result in her emotional fears of being abandoned. Her needs were far more fundamental than I had guessed, being bound up largely with her incapacity to be alone (Winnicott, 1957).

The psychosocial approach helps us to develop a healthy distrust of the obvious. An open mind, imagination and a knowledge of personality functioning, human behaviour and emotional suffering are inherent in the ideas; they assist in reaching 'differential diagnoses and treatment plans'. This is another way of saying that clients interact with their environment in unique ways and if we are to give service which is accurately targeted then, when appropriate, we have to comprehend underlying feelings and motives which can block people from making optimum use of such help. An interesting example is offered by Spurling (1988) of Wendy, a woman who cooperated for a time in his efforts to help her feel less unsatisfied with her life and herself (I shall comment later on what turned out to be a far from straightforward problem). After a couple of visits and missed appointments the client wrote to say that she wanted to try on her own for a while; this was after her past had been mentioned. The letter ended that she would leave it up to him, showing maybe how she wanted help with her past life and was also terrified to do so.

The psychosocial model is usually linked to the writings of Florence Hollis (1964, 1970) though it is one of the oldest of the social work methods, going back as far as the 1930s and even beforehand, to Mary Richmond's (1922) then radical notion of formulating a 'social diagnosis' prior to deciding whether to give indirect treatment (i.e. relieving environmental distress), or direct treatment (i.e. influencing the thoughts and feelings of individuals). Later this became known as the Diagnostic School of social work. Throughout the 1950s and 1960s Freudian psychoanalytic ideas, particularly personality theory, began to feed into what became known as psychodynamic casework: added later were contributions from ego psychology and object-relations theory, known to social workers because of the work of people like John Bowlby.

The 1970s and 1980s saw much emotional and perhaps ill-informed debate about this method of social work. In part, antagonism may have been justified inasmuch as the separate phases of study, diagnosis and treatment may have led to concentrating overmuch on the first two, at the expense of actually doing anything. As indicated in the previous chapter, workers sometimes relied on the client–worker relationship as an end in itself, spending a lot of time with people which research, published in 1976 (Fischer, 1976), suggested was ineffective. Many of the criticisms of psychodynamic casework need, however, to be cautiously analysed: the question of the effectiveness of any treatment process and its relation to change is far from easy.

It might be that, to some degree, the psychosocial approach is less a system of therapy and more an approach to understanding. There are treatment techniques, described by Hollis (1964), as we shall see. But even if we opt for other ways of intervening, if we have tried to make intelligible how people behave and feel, then there is a decreased likelihood of wasting time or dismissing someone as beyond help. As indicated, where we have tried to understand others and ourselves, we may then be able to see underlying reasons for actions – including our own. To return to the work undertaken by Spurling (1988): his persistence with the young woman Wendy became fruitful when eventually he was able to confront his own tentativeness about talking to her about the painful topic of her guilt, shame and anger at having been sexually abused by her father. The safety provided by the worker meant that even though he was male, Wendy did not feel that it was 'interfering' when he helped her to tell the detail of what had happened. And, as the case study concludes, when something is spoken of for the first time in the presence of another, things can never be the same again.

And yet, professionals have to want to hear; if they themselves lack self-awareness, are resistant to getting involved, or if there is fear of 'damaging' others by looking beneath the surface, they are more likely to make mistakes. (Good supervision is invaluable in helping staff to unblock how they feel about clients and letting these feelings be used to guide actions.) Bacon (1988) has shown, for instance, that professionals in child abuse case conferences may operate from a deep-seated, unconscious and collusive rejection of the family (and therefore the child). Social work has to live with the notion that in life there may be 'good' and 'bad'; we may unknowingly choose not to hear or talk about the latter because it is too threatening or because we want to be seen as 'helpful' rather than 'helpless'.

Finally, although I cautioned in earlier chapters about an overuse of the question 'why?', in this approach it would be valid to ponder on why we and those we work with behave in ways which may seem irrational. Clients often ask, 'Why am I like this?' and, when indicated, helping people to remember traumatic incidents from the past or gain insight into the way they function might promote feeling more comfortable about themselves. Moreover, accurate plans for the future may depend on this: when the past is still in the present (Jacobs, 1986) it could prevent progress.

Assessing ego strengths

Basic to the psychosocial approach is a knowledge of psychosexual development (Howe (1987) summarises these ideas in more detail). Freud emphasised the importance of early development, delineating several major stages: oral (first year of life), anal (ages one to three), phallic (ages three to six), latency (ages six to twelve) and genital (continuing from twelve for the rest of life). The origins of faulty personality development were thought to stem from childhood, adjustment problems resulting in unhealthy uses of *ego-defence mechanisms*. These are a further key feature of the psychosocial approach, since defences help individuals to cope with anxiety, thereby preventing the ego from being overwhelmed: they are normal behaviours but they can frustrate coping with reality. Common ego defences are repression, whereby painful thoughts and feelings are excluded from awareness, denial where again the person 'closes their eyes' to threatening actuality but on a more conscious level than repression, and regression, where there is a return to behaviour which is immature. In order to assess how realistic and logical the person is in coping with problems and inner conflicts, i.e. to reveal which method of helping is indicated, then we have to assess this element of personality structure.

According to the psychoanalytic view, the personality consists of three systems: the id, the ego, and the superego which dynamically interact. The impulses originating from the id are governed by the pleasure principle while the 'conscience', the superego strives to inhibit these chaotic drives. The ego, in touch with outer reality, tries to mediate between instincts and the outer environment, thinking through ways of satisfying needs, anticipating consequences and rationally working out solutions. Thus, you can see that if we are to tailor our efforts to each individual's inner and outer needs we need to know if the ego can tolerate self-scrutiny, without being overwhelmed by anxiety; or if probing into the past would not lead to change what level of support the person requires in reducing the stressful demands of their external environment. Moyes (1988) describes a client whom she helped who some might have assessed as being too dependent, anxious and of low intellectual ability to make much use of the psychosocial approach to understanding. However, with verbal and non-verbal methods (board games etc.) the client did gain some insight into unmet childhood needs for security and dependence, and why these were preventing an ability to trust others, to engage in closer relationships and to develop autonomy.

When talking about ego strengths, we are not referring to a fixed condition but to an ever-changing capacity to cope with frustration, control impulses, make mature relationships and use defence mechanisms appropriately. In general, an individual's age, capacity to work through early traumas and the intensity of pressures all affect ego functioning: a truly mature person in this sense is someone who does not need to rely on others for positive self-esteem and who has a deep understanding of who they are. Even if the social worker decides to work on reducing environmental change, as a way of giving hope and comfort to a person who does not desire self-awareness or could not cope with it, it is still useful to be able to gauge ego strengths to see how motivated or reluctant the person is likely to be and what kind of relationship is likely to develop. A fascinating account of working with marital problems in a social services department demonstrated how the two project workers (Mattinson and Sinclair, 1979) were able to sustain and nurture a group of clients whose problems, marital, financial and practical, were related to childhood fears of loss, abandonment and attachment. Drawing on psychodynamic theories, they were able to effect some change in the kinds of referrals which take up a vast amount of agency time, more so when workers do not make an assessment of ego functioning.

When helping adults who appear to have 'infantile' needs, or whose behaviour is baffling (e.g. those who intellectually understand what to do but who do not connect this to their feelings or actions), it might be useful to assess at what stage of psychosexual development they might be stuck. Especially when there has been a past trauma, for instance, loss of a parent at a vulnerable age; then, when there is internal or external pressure, the client frequently regresses to the stage where these earlier issues were not resolved. This is why, in direct work with children, social workers who are skilled in the techniques of this method can help them to regress, revisit painful phases and start to build ego strengths undeveloped in the past. (One such specialist recently told me how useful she finds Bruno Bettelheim's *The Uses of Enchantment* (1988, Penguin Books). Fairy-tales are important in revealing children's anxieties and fantasies and

Bettelheim shows how they help to support and free the child.)

Equally, those clients who seem totally unable to manage their lives (Kaufman, 1966) can be helped to gradually mature with a worker who feels comfortable in a nurturing, restitutive parent–child relationship, where dependency is accepted and worked through. Normally, these are the adults who antagonise agencies because of their neediness and their inability to care for anyone else (until they have been cared for). For example, there is the parent who forgets to have food in the house and who spends the money we give on cigarettes; the patient who is over-concerned with illness but whose numerous tests reveal no abnormality; the person who insists on seeing the social worker at all hours and then is aggressive when limits are imposed. Some time ago Wittenberg (1970) said that

> The caseworker acts as a kind of mother who takes away the mess that the child produces and cleans it up and helps him to do so gradually himself. (p. 155)

With many clients who become stressed by even small matters, such as keeping to an arrangement, we often have to give material things; because verbal communications may have no meaning we have to *show* we care. Lives may have been marked by inconsistency, desertion, the intrusion of too many figures of authority or attacks on self-esteem, we have to provide understanding, holding and containment.

Before moving on to discuss how psychosocial methods have been criticised, I want to emphasise that ego strengths must be assessed before attempting any self-awareness and re-education; particularly when dealing with those who have been diagnosed psychotic or when working with the imma-ture ego of the child, indiscriminate 'laying bare' of feelings can prove overwhelming to the personality and interpreta-tion to aid insight would probably be harmful. Indeed, the immature ego may need help to increase rather than decrease defences to prevent repressed (unconscious) ma-terial from threatening the fragile personality.

110 Social Work Practice

Criticisms of the psychosocial approach

In Britain, the psychosocial approach has been a controversial aspect of social work thought and practice for many years. In 1959, Barbara Wootton's *Social Science and Social Pathology* attacked social caseworkers for posing as miniature psychoanalysts. Wootton declared that, rather than search for underlying reasons for behaviour, the social worker would do better to 'look superficially on top', especially if practical help was sought. Consequently, a great deal of 'looking superficially on top' took place, workers content to provide services and respond to problems as presented. This is frequently all clients want; but for those who had less 'common sense' and easy-to-understand difficulties, there began to be less and less workers trained to spot underlying problems. I have argued, in any case, that even when the goal is service provision, it is beneficial to think about the psychosocial person-in-situation so that resources are not wasted, should latent problems emerge.

The psychosocial approach was so unmercifully denounced in one institution where I taught that it was dropped from the syllabus. There seemed to be a variety of explanations for this. One reason might have been its clinical and obscure jargon; or its tendency to construe cause and effect, often simplistically blaming the past for the present; another the propensity to label clients as inadequate, manipulative or narcissistic whenever they failed to cooperate; research found that clients were angry when workers, unable to give money, refocused their efforts towards intrusive exploration of their personal life (Mayer and Timms, 1970) and there was growing tension between critical sociologists and social work theorists, because the latter ostensibly favoured the status quo rather than struggle, through collective action, to change society.

In addition, when behavioural approaches began to be taught on training courses the results of intervention with specific and overt behaviours could be witnessed and even tested for effectiveness. Comparison between the speed of change using psychosocial support versus behavioural techniques highlighted the utility of the latter (Hudson, 1975).

Furthermore, notions of a therapeutic relationship, self-disclosure, individualisation and self-awareness, plus the power of the worker to make the diagnosis, were antipathetic to the needs of black clients. (Dominelli (1988) in more recent times has suggested that casework 'pathologised' blackness and diverted workers' attention away from racist organisational policies.) Middle-class social workers were criticised by radical sociologists and social policy analysts for concentrating on intrapsychic forces and 'insight giving' while ignoring the effects of harsh, competitive, capitalist systems (Bailey and Brake, 1975). Freud's theories were said to lack a materialist understanding of the individual (Corrigan and Leonard, 1978); so too, one of social work's most experienced practitioners/thinkers, still maintains that the psychosocial school aims to make people fit into a given environment (Jordan, 1987).

Behind the censure of the psychosocial approach and its base in psychoanalytic ideas may lie a presumption that the method is practised by authoritarian caseworkers, who are unable to reflect upon and question what they do. In the past, there may have been rigid believers who could not tolerate ambiguity, diversity and uncertainty about human behaviour, who failed to locate their practice in a socio-economic or linguistic context. Nowadays, most social workers are very much aware that all forms of helping are really forms of power. There are, nevertheless, those who distinguish between 'good' collective struggles to change society and 'bad' individualised, 'conservative' approaches such as the one under discussion here. As I argued in the Introduction, it seems foolish and narrow-minded to opt for an either/or position in one's philosophy and interpretation of 'reality'. (In any event, while radical social workers might be in direct opposition to those who practise 'traditional' social work, my experience is that there can be even more indoctrination and pressure to conform to the radical viewpoint.)

False divisions between private and public worlds ignore the interaction between them. Many attempts have been made to integrate psychoanalysis with various sociological and political theories (see the valuable overview by Pearson *et al.,* 1988). Yelloly (1980), in one of the few books relating to social work and psychoanalysis, using the example of the early days of the women's movement, shows how personal predicaments reflect political existence: psychoanalysis offering insight into the psychological and social chains which keep human beings captive. The same point is made by the feminist psychoanalyst Juliet Mitchell (Mitchell, 1984) who is able to see the value and the drawbacks of a theory which, at one and the same time, implies the inferiority of women and the key to understanding women's psychology and their oppression under patriarchy; critics, moreover, need to realise that psychoanalysis does not begin and end with Freud – it is an active, evolving set of ideas, as Mitchell reminds us.

Nevertheless, it is as well to be mindful of the power of 'received ideas' (Rojek *et al.,* 1988). Rojek and his colleagues have alerted us to the hidden influence of the language of social work: although we use words such as caring and helping, is that what actually happens? Unless we develop self-criticism and the self-awareness I have underlined here, we might unwittingly, by using the techniques which are described in the subsequent section, diminish and demean those we hoped would become 'beings-of-themselves'.

Some benefits and some techniques of the psychosocial approach

Practitioners may be surprised to find that they use some of the psychosocial methods all the time. Much of the 'bread and butter' of our job involves contemplating ideas such as loss, attachment, individual development, anxiety, transference and so on. We find it easy to accept as normal regressed behaviour for instance of those recently bereaved, who are afraid to be alone or who are convinced they have seen or heard their lost loved one. A knowledge of child personality development is a cornerstone for those involved in child care and child guidance work. It is commonplace, also to meet clients who transfer feelings and attitudes on to us that derive from someone else; just as, in countertransference, we unconsciously respond to the client 'as if' we were that person. For example, clients may relate to us as if we are the all-giving, all-powerful parent they need; if we live up to this fantasy we become unable to say no and to be honest about our limitations. A more subtle illustration of transference happened to a residential social worker who winked at one of the young boys in his unit when they were having a meal; the child became hysterical. It transpired that this had reminded the boy of earlier sexual abuse from a swimming instructor.

Olive Stevenson wrote some time ago (1963) how she had applied understanding and skills derived from psychoanalysis to her practice: Jennifer, aged ten, had suffered numerous upheavals in her first years of life; on being refused a chocolate by her foster mother who was ill in bed, Jennifer had destroyed a tray cloth which she had spent months embroidering for her foster parents. They were helped to make sense of what to them was nonsense, the worker explaining that Jennifer's early experience of giving and taking food and of being refused this had acquired emotional significance for her. The child experienced great anxiety when her carer was ill, displayed by infantile, primitive feelings of revenge. The understanding gained by the foster parents prevented possible fostering disruption.

Just when social workers think they are getting somewhere they too might need assistance in supervision to 'stay with' someone who seems to be rejecting their help. Maximé (1986), talks about the confused self-concept and identity of black children reared in care (who have internalised images and feedback that 'black is bad'). These children express rage to others in their environment, especially black social workers, whom they view negatively. Self-rejection through self-destructiveness is another symptom of introjecting (taking in) negative external images of 'black is bad'. Maximé goes on to describe a five-stage process whereby a person can journey through to a secure and confident black identity:

1. The pre-encounter stage where the person's view is white oriented, even denying to themselves that racism exists.
2. The encounter stage where the shattering experience of racism forces the individual to reinterpret their world.

3. Immersion-emersion where the old identity is shed and blackness is intensified, and sometimes deified.
4. Internalisation where the old and new self have separated.
5. Internalisation-commitment when a positive black identity advances so that people love and accept themselves as a black person who can become involved in black groups and black issues.

As hinted, another benefit of the psychosocial approach is that it can assist in supervision (Hawkins and Shohet, 1989); supervisor and supervisee need to understand jointly what is happening in a client–worker relationship. Besides helping the above social worker cope with rejection, there can be space to reflect on 'How does this client make me feel?'. This is not therapy, the boundaries have to be clearly drawn; but it does bring into the session scope for the relationship 'out there' to be mirrored 'in here'. For instance, one student working in Relate yawned throughout supervision when talking about a couple who themselves were bored with their relationship and tired of the 'here we go again' rows they had. (Mattinson, 1975 explores this further.) On a broader front, psychodynamic concepts provide insights into the way that organisations and staff teams work. Simmonds (1988) analysed the defences set up by a group of residential child-care staff whose morale suffered when they could not follow up the young people who had left care to live independently: though this is a real-enough problem the principal issue was that the staff, not wanting to face the loss of the children, never discussed leaving with them and so everyone 'forgot' about the future or planned it somewhat unrealistically.

On this subject, Downes (1988) gives us another edifying case study: Neil, a newly-qualified worker who had been in an area team for four months, had been working for that length of time with a young girl and her baby deemed to be 'at risk'. Despite his colleagues thinking him unrealistic and a 'raw teenager' himself, he was determined to treat the client as a grown-up. The team preferred to be 'giving parents', avoiding hostility thereby. Neil and the client had a huge row when he refused to give in to her demands; the team thought him irresponsible, the motherly receptionist comforted the client who threatened suicide.

Downes analyses the splits between Neil and the client, between Neil and the team and within Neil himself who struggles with himself as a 'sucker or a bastard'. What was missing was a team leader or other manager/supervisor who could have stayed on the boundaries of these dynamics.

Moving on now to consider some of the techniques which may be used. The goal, you will remember, is to assist the person, the situation or both by reducing internal and/or external conflict. Two main procedures are used – sustaining and modifying (see Hollis, 1964).

Sustaining procedures: are those techniques familiar to practitioners who talk about 'offering support' or 'building a relationship.' They include:

Ventilation – this unburdening of feelings and thoughts allows the overwhelmed ego to concentrate on problem solving.

Realistic reassurance – by keeping the person in touch with actuality, not promising what cannot be done, keeping an appraisal of external facts to the forefront etc. the ego's capacity for reality testing is strengthened.

Acceptance in the relationship allows the superego to 'soften'; 'bad' feelings need not be defended against; the person lessens self-criticism, overwork, rigidity, shame at having a problem, and so on.

Logical discussion gives the worker scope to assess someone's ability to reason and confront reality without needing to retreat into fantasy, symptoms of physical illness, pessimism and so on.

Demonstrating behaviour whereby the worker models coping; he/she can be trusted and depended upon being able to tolerate frustration, set limits, keep perspective and to reason – ego strengths a client may need to 'borrow', i.e. copy or internalise, for a time.

Giving information increases the motivation of the ego to handle problem solving, for instance because it sustains hope, separates the facts of what is 'inside' the person and 'outside' in relation to facts and resources and prevents magical expectations.

Offering advice and guidance; in psychosocial terms this enlarges understanding, sustaining the client's own efforts to keep control; reducing doubt and fear of the unknown introduces hope and assists ego capacity for reflection, adaptation and readiness to cope.

Environmental manipulation; helping with rehousing, money, advocacy. Obtaining needed resources, the worker shares the burden of handling practical problems. Reducing anxiety increases self-confidence. (Deprivation produces irrational feelings of shame and guilt; or anger becomes explosive, using up needed, productive mental energy.)

Modifying procedures: these also aim to reduce outer pressures while increasing ego awareness of previously unrecognised aspects of personality dynamics. In social work terms this would be the client gaining insight. Providing that the diagnosis of ego strengths has confirmed that self-scrutiny can be tolerated, techniques include:

Reflective communications to enlarge client's self-understanding: within this is a set of methods which involve sustaining the person while they consider in a new light their opinions, attitudes, behaviour, present feelings, past traumas, early life experiences, using the relationship with the worker as a *corrective emotional experience*.

Confrontation techniques include pointing out patterns of thinking, feeling and doing; for instance, a client who was anxious and trying to come to terms with his homosexuality was confronted with the interpretation that his superego was torturing his ego when the worker suggested, 'It is as if one part of you is persecuting the other'. The client replied, 'That's how it feels'. Confrontation may show clients how they respond in stereotyped ways in their relationships, using an example of the client–worker relationship itself. For example, a person who has had bad experience of dependency could find difficulty accepting anything that the worker says.

Clarification techniques similarly include the use of interpretations to point out, for example, when a person's use of defence mechanisms is getting in the way of change, making them resistant such as, 'Whenever we get around to talking about your father you change the topic'; or the past may inappropriately be influencing the present; for instance, a successful doctor felt very guilty because his father, a car worker, had always been ambitious for another son who became a manual worker. The GP felt he had betrayed his father who had always said, 'You'll go nowhere, like me.'

Interpretation, as implied, is a major procedure; usually it comprises an observation which helps the person to link their present circumstances in their lives 'out there' to the feelings that they have 'in here', that is, the relationship with the helper to what went on 'back there', the past (Jacobs, 1986). This forms a 'triangle of conflict', an example of which would be a person unable to stay in any job without becoming resentful and challenging towards female managers: the worker might interpret, 'You say you get anxious with women in authority. I remember you saying your mother was the boss at home. I wonder if you feel worried now because I am a woman who seems to be telling you what to do?' Similarly, interpretations might be necessary when symptoms are used as a diversion away from painful conflicts in life and in an individual's inner world: thus, those who treat eating disorders such as anorexia and bulimia interpret these as fear of feeling emotionally empty or wanting to get rid of one's badness; they offer, in one-to-one and self-help group relationships, the chance to talk about these 'baby' needs (see Dana and Lawrence, 1988).

While there is some doubt about the effectiveness of this kind of interpretation (insight does not necessarily lead to change), you can see that these methods are often no more than a reflective discussion helping to answer 'why am I like this?'

The techniques do not aim to elucidate unconscious motives, restructure personalities or use skills such as the analysis of dreams, free association and the rest. We do not have the time, the training or clients' permission to do this. 'Archaeological digging' into the past is not necessary either, since all we are hoping for is that the person might see things a little differently and feel that they have more control over their problems in the present.

Framework for understanding the psychosocial approach

Theoretical base is that of Freudian personality theory, with an emphasis on the ego's capacity for adaptation and problem solving. Building on this, Erikson (1965) has analysed human growth and development bringing in the importance of psychosocial transitions ('Eight Stages of Man' [*sic*]), whereby he integrates social factors with intrapsychic ones throughout the human life-span. Hollis (1970) suggests that the interplay between the 'psycho' and the social aspects would merit calling this a systems approach, Important concepts include defence mechanisms, personality structure, transference and countertransference, resistance and early trauma.

Problems are either intrapsychic, interpersonal or environmental ones. They relate to meeting basic needs, e.g. love, trust, dependence, separateness and autonomy. Problems can be unconscious in origin, the 'cause' of a problem, the 'why?' is seen as important.

Goals are to understand and change the person, the situation or both, that is, direct and indirect intervention. Specific, proximate goals help people with focused aspects of their lives, while ultimate goals might be more vague and relate to self-understanding.

Client's role is somewhat passive, a patient role almost. Where indicated, the person talks about thoughts and feelings and by bringing them into the open or into conscious awareness, begins to understand themselves better.

Worker's role is to study, diagnose and treat the 'person-in-situation' whole; the worker may or may not share the assessment with the client, dependent on the client's ego capacity for self-understanding (This can be viewed as professional omnipotence, since we can never know all there is to know about someone's history or the workings of their mind.) Treatment processes include establishing a relationship, building ego support via the client's identification with the worker's strengths, helping the client to grow in terms of identity and self-awareness and working through previously unsettled inner conflicts. A major contribution is obtaining needed practical resources and advocating with others to reduce pressure such that personality change may occur.

Techniques. Two main procedures are used, sustaining and modifying. The former sustains the ego via techniques such as demonstrating coping behaviour and listening (to encourage ventilation). The latter is used with sustaining procedures and involves the use of confrontation, clarification and interpretation.

Case example

A female probation officer was the third person to be assigned to supervise Joan who, despite a social enquiry report recommendation for a conditional discharge for a first offence (stealing a social security cheque), had been placed under a two-year probation order. Previous probation officers had assessed Joan as a 'soft touch' for everyone in her street who used her as an unpaid baby-sitter and general dog's-body.

Joan was nineteen, unemployed and the eldest of a large, working-class family living in poverty. Following her mother's death when she was eleven, Joan's father had remarried and had five more children. Joan and her stepmother were not close; the latter frequently borrowed and did not repay money lent by her stepdaughter. The client had stolen the cheque on behalf of an older woman friend and had not gained personally from the crime.

Joan seemed to have a low opinion of herself; her appearance was unkempt and she looked about thirteen years old. The probation officer, rather than encourage the woman to leave home as previous workers had done, decided instead to see what she could do to raise the client's self-esteem and relieve her feelings of depression. It was important to realise that Joan's social circumstances, not simply her personality in terms of ego functioning, had contributed to the offence: also, Joan, at that time, wanted to stay near to her father since, in some respects, he provided stability in her life. The psychosocial diagnosis thus incorporated an assessment, not merely of the client's possible immaturity (probably exacerbated by a lack of opportunity to get work and achieve what Erikson (1965) calls 'industry' versus 'inferiority'), but also her status as a woman, the somewhat sexist approach of the organisation in pushing her to leave home, the culture of the community in which many deprived people lived and the ego support provided by her father.

The worker's efforts, accordingly, were both direct intervention and indirect intervention in the community. A home visit confirmed father's backing, though Joan's stepmother, needing help with the rearing of five young children, tended to compete with Joan for father's attention. He seemed to be something of a 'pig-in-the-middle', not knowing whose side to take whenever Joan and his wife argued. The probation officer planned to ask for an early discharge of the probation order and to raise in a team meeting the department's approach to female clients, which sometimes stereotyped them as irresponsible and inadequate.

In her direct work with Joan, she explored the client's preconceptions of what the contact would entail. Having been controlled to some extent previously and not wanting to depend on the worker who was perceived as a strong person, Joan eventually admitted that these were her fears. All her life she had been pushed around and she expected this from the probation officer; in any case, she had been compelled into the relationship and had negative feelings about it. Ventilation of these feelings brought them into the open where they seemed less threatening and also they could be talked about from a reality, rather than fantasy basis.

The probation officer spent some time in subsequent meetings giving information about services and benefits and clarifying with the client about what should be their aims. These discussions increased Joan's motivation to see her needs as important as anyone else's and to realise that the worker was not the 'fount of wisdom' since Joan knew more than she about welfare systems, job opportunities and the like. Deliberate ego building on the part of the worker, who described Joan's helpfulness towards others as 'good and bad' and not merely a symptom of not being assertive enough, let Joan reconsider her own behaviour in a less rigid light. She had always swallowed other's opinions that she was a 'soft touch', lowering her self-regard. In actual fact, she liked baby-sitting and looking after children, it was not just a case of being unable to say 'no'.

Nevertheless, a few weeks later, Joan was arrested for non-payment of the fine; she had entrusted this money to her stepmother who had spent it. She felt guilty about having to explain all this and reluctant to challenge her stepmother about it. With the worker's help, this was sorted out, but in a way which modelled for Joan how it is not selfish to say what you want and yet that for women it may be a harder thing to do.

At first, in the relationship, the worker accepted Joan's statement that she had got over her mother's death easily and that she had liked her father's new wife for a while. Later, however, Joan felt safe enough to admit to the worker (and to herself) how sad and angry she had actually felt. The lowering of these defence mechanisms in an atmosphere of acceptance, released pent up thoughts and feelings of loss, abandonment, jealousy and rage, which the probation officer was able to contain; they discussed how natural these childlike fears were, even though, on occasion, Joan's anger was directed towards her, especially when there was a need to reinforce the statutory requirements of the probation order.

The worker consciously used herself as a role model, being a woman and coming from the same sort of social background. At this stage, Joan began to identify with her helper, talking and dressing like her. This apparent dependency did not worry the probation officer who anticipated the later stage of 'separation-individuation'; like the child who moves away from the parent but likes to go back for approval and comfort, in some ways we all retain traces of childhood needs. It was agreed that Joan would help the probation officer at a camp for youngsters, since Joan eventually wanted to work with children and this was a chance to get some experience. This helped her to gain a firmer sense of her own identity as the teenagers enjoyed her company.

As the ending phase loomed, Joan's father bought her a record player to replace one that had been stolen. This prompted his daughter to reflect with the worker, in a mature fashion, how awkward it must be for him and her stepmother to cope with their income and how he might feel torn between the needs of his daughter and his wife. The relationship with the worker at times resembled Joan's split between her anger at her stepmother and her admiration for her mother, being at times aggressive and at others cooperative towards the helper. This could have been confusing for both parties if some insight and understanding had not been gained. By the time the supervision order was discharged Joan had a much clearer idea of who she was; she rediscovered her sense of humour, which, living in an area of increasing unemployment, she would probably have to hang on to. She turned down the worker's offer of a place in a women's group she was planning, preferring to help herself.

6

Behavioural Social Work

Why is it that behaviour therapy programmes (formerly known as behaviour modification), which usually aim to change overt behaviours, are couched in difficult language? Given the simplicity that behaviour is learned and unlearned we have to grapple with words such as modelling, observation, learning, imitation, social learning and vicarious learning – all of which mean the same thing! We are fortunate that educators such as Sheldon and Hudson, whose work is referred to here, have helped to make the concepts relevant and accessible to social work. Learning theory, on which behavioural principles are based, is a vast, well-researched field. Therefore the objectives of this chapter will be limited to exploring four types of learning, describing some techniques and procedures, and, because it is of growing interest to social workers, taking the cognitive-behaviour therapy perspective and examining it in some detail.

Four types of learning

A social worker who bases their practice on aspects contained in the previous chapter would say that behaviour, thoughts, attitudes and feelings are influenced largely by the past and by internal conflict: the theorist responsible for developing behaviourism, B.F Skinner, who died in 1990, would have contested this saying that behaviour and personality are determined mainly by current events in the external environment. The behavioural approach to therapy grew rapidly in the 1950s and 1960s, partly to get away from the dominance of the psychoanalytic perspective: in some ways, it resembles the task-centred approach in that it is focused on a particular problem, specific procedures are followed and time limits are imposed. *Respondent* (classical) and *operant* conditioning were developed in work with animals: the former explained simple reflex behaviours such as blinking when a light flashes; the latter model, developed by Skinner, examined non-reflexive, active, trial-and-error learning. Experiments on *Observational learning* showed that we also learn by watching other people; *cognitive learning*, more recently, suggests that private self-talk and thoughts govern our behaviour too. Let us take each of these four types of learning in turn.

1. *Respondent conditioning,* Howe (1987) gives an amusing set of examples which help to illustrate how behaviour which is out of conscious control can become controlled. He reminds us that Pavlov's dogs were taught to salivate at the sound of a tuning fork just before food was presented; thus the stimulus that evoked the response (fork sound) became the conditioned stimulus and the saliva the conditioned response. Textbooks represent this as S → R.

The stimulus of a dog biting an unwary social worker will evoke a fear response, resulting perhaps in the worker avoiding all the places where dogs may lurk (in this event, the dog stimulus has widened and become *generalised* to a fear of all dogs). In other words, something happens and a specific *response* occurs. This gives a clue, moreover, to how the connection might be broken in therapy. Systematic desensitisation (also called reciprocal inhibition) is based on this principle of respondent conditioning. It is used primarily for anxiety and avoidance reactions. Having assessed the stimuli that provoke anxiety, relaxation techniques are taught and the client helped to establish an 'anxiety hierarchy'. So, for example, a person who is afraid to leave the house will be asked to rank which situations they find easy and which most difficult when trying to go outdoors. While the client relaxes, each situation, say from putting out the milk bottles to going to the shops, is imagined progressively up the 'ladder' of feeling. *In vivo*, that is real life experience, is probably one familiar to education social workers who may help a pupil to return to school by gradually getting used to the bus route, the playground and finally the classroom with the other children.

2. *Operant conditioning*. This consists of actions that operate on the environment to produce consequences. The key feature is that behaviour is altered by its consequences. If the changes brought about by the behaviour are reinforcing (i.e. bring about a reward or eliminate something unpleasant for the person) then there is more chance that that behaviour will occur again. Thus, operant behaviour therapy has been useful in returning long-stay hospital patients to the community, because token economy systems and verbal praise rewarded desired behaviour such as self-help and social skills and reduced unwanted, bizarre actions. Unlike insight giving and the psychoanalytic approach, this method has been found appropriate for people who are diagnosed psychotic, since no interpretation of 'why' the behaviour occurs is necessary. (See Sheldon (1984) for further examples of this method with those who are mentally ill.)

Positive reinforcement, known as the ABC of behaviour (Hudson and MacDonald, 1986), is most useful for social workers, especially those dealing with parents whose children misbehave. Parents find it fascinating to discover that they may inadvertently have been reinforcing the 'wrong' behaviour. Thus, the child screams and gets a sweet to keep him/her quiet: this behaviour is more likely to occur again because of the reward. To understand the sequence of events it is necessary to examine the Antecedents of the Behaviour and its Consequences (ABC).

This is shown diagrammatically below.

Antecedents	Behaviour	Consequences
Mother Sweet Refusal	Child screams	Receives sweet

An important aspect of giving reinforcers, for example in encouraging young offenders in treatment centres to clear away their games, is that the reward, say a smile or thanks from the staff, should be given *immediately* and *consistently* by the whole team until such behaviour is occurring naturally and need not be so systematically commented upon (because the reward tends to lose some of its value over time). Here, 'correct' behaviour is rewarded and undesirable behaviour ignored. Using a visual aid to record positive gains such as 'star charts' can reward achievements. Randall (1990) used a similar device to boost an elderly person as she began to successfully do household chores.

Chaining and backward chaining are operant procedures too; they can be used to teach new behaviours and have been successful in work with people with learning difficulties (Tsoi and Yule, 1982). Teaching self-help skills such as dressing or brushing one's teeth is not as simple as it sounds, though, because each successive step to achieve such behaviour has to be separately analysed and progressively tracked. As an example: backward chaining was used by foster parents to teach their foster son, who had a learning difficulty, to make his own bed. The foster mother performed all but the last link in the chain, then reinforced the child for carrying out the last step of tucking in the sheet. Then the last two links were left for him to master, and so on backwards. He needed a lengthy programme but eventually gained the satisfaction of fully completing the tasks himself.

The termination of something unpleasant is called negative reinforcement (not to be confused with punishment) and is aimed at reinforcing wanted behaviour, so that children may keep quiet if only to avoid the pain of being shouted at. This strategy is not as welcome as a positive reward because it does little to increase new behaviour and shouting can sometimes become rewarding when some attention is preferred to none. A combined strategy is preferred if the aim is to decrease or extinguish unacceptable behaviour; accordingly, when staff in a unit for disabled people wanted to stop a ten-year-old girl from whining, they collectively ignored her when she whined and played bubbles and gave her a much loved mirror when she was quiet.

'Time out' (that is, from reinforcement), is an extinction procedure which, when used properly and ethically, can be successful. (I know of some agencies who mistakenly control aggressive behaviour by isolating people for lengthy periods – this is not time out but dubious punishment.) The procedure should follow within seconds of the misbehaviour, clear explanations should have been given in advance about what would happen and why, and the person should be taken to a time out area, such as the corner of the room where there are no pleasant distractions or harmful objects for between three and five minutes. When working with groups of parents whose children were 'driving them up the wall', Scott (1983) found it necessary to keep parents motivated by using humour (a relaxation technique, in essence), teaching them the 'when . . . then' technique ('When you have cleared away your toys then you can watch television'), modelling the use of praise and time out and, most importantly, warning that target behaviours usually get worse before they get better!

3. *Observational learning.* By copying what other people do we can learn something without having to go through a process of trial and error. Bandura (1977) says that there are three different effects of what is known as modelling: we can learn new skills or ideas; social skills can be imitated and practised and fear responses can be inhibited, e.g. sitting next to someone on a plane who enjoys the experience. The main difference from the previous two types of learning is that reinforcement is not viewed as essential. Learning can be deliberate, such as the groups set up to teach social skills or assertiveness via role play and video films; or it can be unplanned, when, for instance, clients copy the way we talk to social security officials on the telephone. Imitative learning is even more likely when there is a good working relationship or where the model is perceived as competent and of high status. Black staff in nurseries for black children (see Morgan, 1986) are deliberately chosen to counter images of white people as superior; play materials which portray successful black people, music, art and literature provide positive symbolic models for the children.

4. *Cognitive learning* Traditionally, learning theory has been concerned with outward behaviour, fixing people as passive beings whose behaviour can be altered by environ-

mental controls. However, it has been recognised by cognitive behaviourists that we also feel and think, that we attach
meaning to events. Bandura's work, mentioned above,
paved the way inasmuch as some kind of internalisation of
images can influence behaviour. Beck (1989) made a major
contribution; working with depressed and emotionally disordered people he suggested that negative thoughts about
themselves, their situation and their prospects brought
about their emotional disorders. In the same way, Meichenbaum (1978) suggested that the way that we talk to ourselves, 'inner speech', affects our behaviour, Thus, if we
keep telling ourselves that we will not cope, there is a
likelihood that we will not.

However, in an excellent book on this topic (Scott, 1989),
Mike Scott reminds us that the idea that thought processes
can have an impact on emotions and behaviour is not a new
one. Readers may be familiar with Kelly's Personal Construct Theory (Kelly, 1955) which showed how people
construct their own view of the world, and Ellis's (Ellis,
1962) Rational Emotive Therapy (RET) which maintains
that we upset ourselves by our irrational thoughts – we are
upset, not by events, but by the view we take of them.
Modern cognitive-behaviour therapy incorporates ideas
from Kelly and Ellis: as a social worker, Scott has found
these theories to be appropriate when working with depression, anxiety, marital work and work with children. The
processes used in the practice of cognitive-behaviour therapy will be explored in some detail towards the end of this
chapter.

Some techniques and procedures

Really we ought to talk about behaviour therapies because
this perspective encompasses a variety of ways of changing
behaviour and increasing the number of response options
(i.e. new skills). It is an action-oriented approach; people
are helped to take a specific action to change observable
behaviour; goals are spelled out in concrete terms and the

procedure is almost scientifically evaluated by questioning what was done, how often, by whom, for what specific problem and under which particular circumstances. In the cognitive field, private or subjective meanings are the key to a person learning to understand how their cognitions (thoughts) have distorted reality and how, therefore, the individual has the responsibility and the capacity to unravel disturbances, regardless of their origin.

In comparison to the psychosocial approach, the client selects goals, the relationship is seen as important but not sufficient to achieve change, work is a joint effort, a written plan of action may be signed and the worker functions typically as a teacher who helps the client to understand the method to perpetuate self-help. The past is not seen as important; neither is the 'why', that is the 'cause' of problem pursued.

The initial stage of work is to do a behavioural assessment. This is a detailed account of exactly what happens before, during and after a problematic event. The client may keep a diary so that all the factors which could affect outcomes are taken into account. Next, the client says which behaviour is to be increased/decreased. The worker clarifies who or what else in the environment could assist or prevent the change effort (for instance sometimes a partner might subtly reinforce a woman's drinking pattern; slippery floors and high toilets can deter elderly people from using the toilet). Each goal is framed in behavioural terms: as with task-centred practice, it is insufficient to say something like, 'John will do as his parents tell him'. Far better to state that John will be home by 9 p.m. during the week and 10 p.m. at weekends, what the reward will be and what will happen if he arrives later.

A handout or explanatory leaflet may sustain the person's efforts: in challenging depressive thoughts a client may complete a sheet recording thoughts; the emotions these aroused; the automatic dysfunctional thought that accompanied this, such as 'I am worthless'; what rational thought response they tried and the degree of success they achieved. Or it could be that the strategy is to increase a person's behavioural repertoire; for instance helping to assert oneself with an authority figure, the techniques would follow the following steps:

1. Identify what behaviour is to be learned.
2. Instruct or demonstrate what this behaviour looks like.
3. Ask the person to role play or copy the behaviour.
4. Provide feedback and reward desired responses.
5. Rehearse and practise again, modelling again if necessary.
6. Desired behaviour may need to be shaped gradually using praise.
7. Assign homework – 'practice makes perfect'.
8. Evaluate 'before and after' ratings of the behaviour.

The chaper on working with groups gives more guidance with this particular form of training.

There are critics of this method, those who would argue that it is unethical to control or 'disrespect' people. Hudson and MacDonald (1986) counter by showing how the use of influence permeates social work methods of all types. They show that behavioural work is usually effective because it is prepared to measure what is achieved and engages the client on overt behaviour which they choose to change, not covert goals which the worker thinks would be 'good' for them. I think too that being prepared to share our skills with clients, teaching them what we do so that we are dispensable, is something we could do more of.

The growth of cognitive-behaviour therapy

As stated earlier, the field of cognitive-behaviour therapy owes much to the work of the late George Kelly (1955). (an interesting account of how personal constructs and personal change occur during social work training, using Kelly's ideas, is given by Tully, 1976.) We each bring 'theories' about the world, unique ways of anticipating events and relationships, which colour our cognitive processes. Equally, Albert Ellis's (1962) work attempted to show that people's aberrations in thinking, such as self-defeating beliefs, create disturbances in the way we feel about things: he would propose that if someone is unhappy after a divorce, it is not the divorce itself which causes this but the person's *beliefs* about being a failure or losing a partner, or whatever. Beck's application of these ideas to treating depression (see Beck, 1989) in the 1970s, contributed significantly to the growth of the cognitive-therapy movement. He developed a system of psychotherapy which helped people to overcome their blindspots and the way they reacted to situations: he educated them to understand their cognitive styles and underlying cognitive structures (or unconscious philosophies) which were activated by particular events.

He used many methods to correct erroneous beliefs – an *intellectual* approach, which identified misconceptions, tested how valid these were and then substituted more appropriate concepts; an *experiential* approach, which motivated people to powerfully experience situations which could modify assumptions, and a *behavioural* approach which encouraged the development of new coping techniques, for instance, systematic desensitisation procedures described earlier. So, he worked not only on clients' thoughts but on outward behaviour and feelings. Most practitioners term the approach cognitive-behavioural, nowadays, to illustrate that problem reduction involves a wide variety of modalities.

For a time, critics pointed out that workers seemed to ignore clients' stories and how they felt: films of Albert Ellis show him humourously disputing clients' philosophies and crisply dismissing the importance of their early history (unlike Rogers' counselling methods which we explored in Chapter 2, he relentlessly repeats that, 'You feel bad because you *think* it's bad'). However, sensitivity and acceptance are seen as part of the therapeutic alliance, though having pinned someone down to a few goals, the techniques could involve rapid-fire questions which try to reveal the absurdity and self-destructiveness of those irrational 'shoulds' and 'oughts'. However, Beck (1989) warns against dogmatism and ignoring when clients disagree; he ensures that his interpretation is accepted saying, 'You've heard my view of the problem, what do you think of it?'. If there are reservations the person is encouraged to offer other interpretations and consider the consequences of their ideas.

The stages which are followed in cognitive-behaviour therapy are:

1. *Engagement.* The client's expectations of help are explored in a leisurely fashion, conveying the message that there is time to listen and that the worker cares. The use of open questions allows the person to talk freely.
2. *Problem focus.* Having identified some problems that could be targeted for exploration, the worker asks, 'Which problems do you most want help with?', i.e. prioritise.
3. *Problem assessment.* Here one specific example is examined in detail. The client is asked to describe an event, their underlying assumptions or inferences from it, their feelings, thoughts and behaviours towards the event and, 'In what ways would you like to feel, think and behave differently than you do now?', i.e. goals.
4. *Teach cognitive principles* and practices of the therapy and get the person to look at their own thoughts; for example, teach them to spot when they use the words 'should' and 'ought', 'I should (not) have done that' or 'I ought to feel guilty' etc.
5. *Dispute and challenge* these target assumptions.
6. *Encourage client's self-disputing* through the use of questions. For instance, 'What evidence do you have? Is there another way of looking at this? Are your thoughts logical?'
7. *Set behavioural homework* to carry on this process and keep a diary of distorted inferences and self-evaluations.
8. *Ending.* Teach self-therapy to maintain improvement.

Currently, within the cognitive-behaviourist arena, there is acknowledgement that 'thought' is a much more complicated notion: the study of the relationship between thought and language has long been studied by Chomsky, a professor of philosophy and linguistics. Chomsky, in a critique of behavioural psychology, says that we are not a lump of clay, shaped by punishment and reward, otherwise how is it that very young children, without being taught deliberately, master the complexities of language (see Magee, 1982; Lyons, 1977)? In other words, there is probably an intimate relationship between the deep structure of language and the workings of the mind. We almost come full circle again to Kelly's theories of how we each construct our worlds.

Framework for understanding behavioural approaches

Theoretical base is learning theory, which includes respondent and operant conditioning, observational and cognitive learning.

Problems which respond well to this approach include phobias, habits, anxiety, depression and obsessive-compulsive disorders (perhaps with drug treatment in tandem). Also, behavioural deficits, such as social skills are treated through behavioural regimes.

Goals are specific, observable (or self-reported in the case of something like a sexual difficulty). Goals must be stated in behavioural terms.

The client's role The person helps to measure the baseline behaviour, its frequency, intensity, duration and the context within which it occurs (see Sheldon, 1983). Diaries and other records may be kept. The client's view of what is a reward for them is vital, as are their goals for change. The person usually must be motivated or helped to be motivated (for instance, Scott, 1989, suggests that those with drinking problems must be at the stage where negative consequences are acknowledged). Where a child is the client, the carer or other change agent needs to be motivated.

The worker's role is to help with the behavioural assessment and to mobilise any necessary resources. A contract may be drawn up. Strategies must be capable of being evaluated and measured for effectiveness. A concerned, genuine and hopeful relationship is necessary, if not sufficient, for change. The worker is active, directive, challenging and an educator.

Techniques include systematic desensitisation, extinction procedures and positive reinforcement, teaching self-control and thought-stopping techniques, disputing irrational thoughts and giving information to other agents such as teachers, parents and colleagues involved in the programme.

Case example using cognitive-behaviour therapy

The following referral was dealt with by a student on placement in a psychiatric day hospital. The student, whom I shall call Jim, had studied behavioural ideas and was trying some of the procedures used in cognitive-behaviour therapy for the first time.

Mr Lin was a fifty-year-old, happily married man with grown-up children. He was twice made redundant from his factory jobs and, just as he was about to return to employment, he became increasingly depressed. Eventually, he was admitted to the day hospital where a multidisciplinary assessment revealed that he had been experiencing an array of problems – behavioural, cognitive, affective and physical. His symptoms included depression, feelings of unreality, fears of dying and loss of confidence. The multidisciplinary team, being an open and creative one, agreed that Jim could take a key part in the treatment regime.

Mr Lin agreed to see the student who explained about anxiety management techniques (Meichenbaum, 1978) and Beck's approach to cognitive therapy. They agreed to meet weekly for the duration of the placement and follow what these programmes suggested, with Mr Lin completing homework tasks in between. He had to learn to relax using an audiotape, keep a record of his upsetting thoughts and measure how much success he had in replacing these with more realistic ones. Because depressed people find it hard to do anything active or pleasurable, Mr Lin was reassured that any change was for the good, so even filling in the thought record was a huge achievement, which would also break the monotony of his routine. Scott (1989) tells his clients that depression is like the mind hanging out a sign that it is 'temporarily out of order' or, 'the mind going on strike for better pay and conditions'.

The multidisciplinary assessment had not revealed a history of suicide attempts or impulsivity and so the student introduced anxiety-provoking role play situations in some sessions, restoring the client's loss of confidence in getting on a bus. Together they read out aloud leaflets on coping with depression; they practised the techniques of relaxation together. Other anxiety management techniques included reminding Mr Lin that his feelings of faintness and palpitations did not mean he was about to have a heart attack, as the medical report had ruled out organic disorders. He began to recognise that they are the body's normal reactions to stress and tension and are not dangerous in themselves – when encouraged to visualise a feared event and become tense, he felt how his body tensed. He was taught to wait for the fear to pass, not to fight or give way to it, to just 'accept it'. Mr Lin realised that his fear faded if he stopped adding to it with the fear of fear itself.

Regular practice at home speeded up recovery; he looked more hopeful with each week that passed. But the student gave him advice to 'go slow' and to expect setbacks, recommending these as an extra chance to practise. The word 'practise' was used deliberately rather than that of 'test' as the latter is daunting and can result in clients brooding on failure, rather than accepting that life is made up of good days and bad days, that recovery is 'two steps forward and one back'.

To show Mr Lin that he might be upsetting himself because of self-defeating thought patterns, Jim gave him a list to keep of the ten most common negative thoughts:

1. All or nothing thinking – seeing everything in black and white.
2. Overgeneralisation – one bad experience leads to constant bad luck.
3. Mental filter – dwelling on the bad and filtering out the positive.
4. Automatic discounting – brushing aside compliments, 'He's just being nice'.
5. Jumping to conclusions such as mind reading and fortune telling; 'I know he doesn't like me; the future holds nothing.'
6. Magnification and minimisation, the binocular trick of blowing things up or shrinking them out of proportion.
7. Emotional reasoning that, 'I feel guilty therefore I must have done something bad'.

8. Should statements – 'I should do this' or 'I must . . .' produces guilt rather than motivation.
9. Labelling and mislabelling one*self* as a failure rather than what you *did* was a failure.
10. Personalisation – whatever happens, assuming it is your fault.

Mr Lin could identify himself in these statements. As an example of 'picking on himself', he remembered doing some carpentry in the day hospital workshop which turned out unsatisfactory but which he magnified as 'disastrous'. Low self-worth is often central in depression; therapists using this approach often use the following challenge: when Mr Lin would describe himself as worthless, the worker would query this saying, 'If one of your family got depressed would you think they were worthless?' 'Definitely not', the client would reply to which the worker would respond, 'So is there a law for you and another one for other people?' Mr Lin eventually recovered. Therapies such as these have been positively evaluated (Scott and Stradling, 1990) and doubt-less will feature regularly in attempts at offering community-based care in the future.

7

Working with Families

Working with children and families continues to be a high priority for social services departments, especially with the introduction of the Children Act of 1989. Many of the referrals are for practical help or are part of statutory work aimed at protecting and controlling this client group (see Jones, 1983). Sometimes referrals turn up difficulties rooted in unsatisfactory family relationships and this is the focus of this chapter. While only a minority of referrals are said to be 'marital' ones, that is, conflicting partners, on close examination such interpersonal problems lie at the heart of many other difficulties (Mattinson and Sinclair, 1979). This is a compelling reason for promoting working with couples as well.

For some years social work with families was known as 'family casework' (Jordan, 1972) and, if ever the whole family was seen together, this was intended to better the welfare of one of its members. In the past thirty years, 'family therapy' has become an accepted approach: this is more than doing 'casework with more people in the room', it is used when the whole family is the client and the target for change. When one or more family members are having difficulties this is thought to be a cause and a consequence of interaction. People affect and are affected by one another and so it is necessary to see how people get along with each other and, more fundamentally, how the family solves its problems. This is an important part of the assessment, giving an indication also how dysfunction might be prevented.

Although there has been dismay at calling these methods of practice 'marital and family therapy', with connotations of clinical work and learning 'tricks of the trade' (Whan, 1983),

I shall refer to them as such, merely for convenience. I have no time for parading skills or using the family as entertainment, which was the style of a few early 'followers' of this movement. Down-to-earth workers have shown that the ideas can be used practically and in a range of settings (Treacher and Carpenter, 1984). Strategies for change which are employed with humanity and humility (Walrond-Skinner, 1979) can help families and couples to draw on their own problem-solving solutions and strengths.

Understanding family dynamics

Family trends in the 1990s and the diversity of family life from a race and class perspective make it impossible to advise what is a 'conventional family': quoting research from the Family Policy Studies Centre, Jervis (1990) shows that cohabitation, children born outside of marriage, lone parent families, stepfamilies and dual working couples are increasingly becoming the norm. Each family differs in the way members communicate, their values and their structural relationships. Although we all have a picture of how families behave and their composition, this stems very much from our experiences in our family of origin. When trying to understand family dynamics there is a danger, therefore, that, if we are from the same ethnic group or class, that we assume we have a lot in common. Trying to replicate our own family style with client families is another trap for the unwary.

For example, O'Brian (1990) gives the following account of trying to engage a Bangladeshi family whose fifteen-year-old daughter had not attended school because her father objected to the school and to the need for her to have any formal education. Being from the same minority ethnic group, O'Brian said, 'Look Mr M. I know what it is like living in this country and having to accept its rules and regulations. We are both foreigners here and I understand what it is like for you.' Mr M replied, 'Sir, with the greatest respect you are not the same as us.' The girl's father went on to say that it had nothing to do with different religions either – it was that the social worker was in a position of authority. Similarly, a colleague of mine, one of three brothers, was working with a family of the same composition. Despite having many years experience in family therapy, he began to behave as if he were one of the brothers. Whenever I work with a family where the father stays in a peripheral role, I try to watch that I do not recreate a mirror image of my own family's functioning. (Bowen (1978) believes that, before working intensively with other people's families, we should sort out our own!) Thus, it is as well not to generalise but to try to understand: 'How does *this* family work?'

Trying to understand a family is like jumping on to a moving bus: you have the disadvantage of being a temporary passenger on their journey through a stage in their life, with people leaving and joining along the way. Like an individual who copes with transitions and life crises, as we saw in Chapter 3, families go through a life cycle. But it is a much more awkward business, because at each phase in their development the whole group has to reshuffle, while at the same time providing stability and continuity for its members. Gorell Barnes (1984) deals with this concept of the family life cycle, explaining what happens when we leave home, achieve independence, become half of a couple, have children, face an 'empty nest', become dependent and so on.

Such changes are made all the more demanding as each member is probably struggling with their individual life stages at the same time: a woman who has launched children and achieved independence may be faced with her mother who is having to adjust to dependence, perhaps on this same daughter. All the time, families are losing members and gaining members, making space for maybe competing needs, renegotiating the numerous patterns of relationship between people – this is why referrals often have life-cycle changes at the nub of what is going wrong.

According to Gorell Barnes (1984), families can be placed at one of three possible points on a spectrum from flexibility, through rigidity to chaos. Years ago, Jordan (1972) illuminatingly described families which were difficult to break free from as 'integrative' and those whose members were segregated and went their separate ways as 'centrifugal': Minuchin later (1974) termed these patterns of closeness and distance 'enmeshed' and 'disengaged'. These ideas may help us to assess if a family can 'bend' with its changing membership and processes (for instance, if there is adaptability of rules when a child enters adolescence): also, albeit that there are different cultural norms, to enquire if a family is able to regulate their boundaries and can tolerate closeness and distance, dependence and independence.

Another useful concept which helps to understand how families act is to see it as a system, a set of interacting parts with a particular purpose. Families may have subsystems which comprise the marital subsystem, the children subsystem, the sibling subsystem, mother–daughter and father–son subsystems and so on. The family's relationship to outside, wider systems, i.e. the suprasystem is as important to understand as their internal dynamics. The case study of Paula in Chapter 2 revealed a woman who was struggling to bring up two children in a disadvantaged environment; other families in the street were so used to social workers entering and defining their lives that they were viewed as 'one of the family'; workers often found families outside in the street sorting out one another's problems until 'their' social worker arrived. With limited understanding, an assessment could be made which inferred that Paula and families such as this had 'boundary' problems, that is, allowed external systems to overly influence their internal dynamics. But, unfortunately, that is the reality for some. (When working with children to prepare them for new families, Redgrave (1987) often found the social worker painted in as part of the family group.)

In the same way, O'Brian (1990) points out that the suprasystem cannot be ignored when working with black families – racism affects every aspect of their lives. It helps, therefore, to see the family as an open system in transformation, constantly changing in relation to internal and external forces. Occasionally families 'get stuck', maybe as the result of coping with their own internal crises or because the agencies with which they interact over-react (Coulshed and Abdullah-Zadeh, 1985). When this happens, solutions become part of a problem spiral. For example, services some-times are dependent on someone being given a label, such as 'a violent family'; in one family the education service managed to gain the attention of the social services by labelling an unhappy boy as an 'arsonist', although the actual event was a fire in a waste-paper basket.

Environmental circumstances are a large part of the assessment of family dynamics, if only to ensure that all our efforts are not unravelled once a person returns to the context in which difficulties arose. In one agency, I was shown an enormous file of a family where every member had received individual programmes of help for over twenty years. Each time anyone returned to the fold, from residen-tial assessment or care, their problems returned with them.

A further tool which can assist in understanding family dynamics and which has also been used with adoptive and foster families is the genogram; otherwise known as the family tree, it depicts relationship patterns and events over generations. Births, deaths, divorce, crises and other signifi-cant life events can be recorded briefly. A lengthy 'case' presentation or several pages of social history can be con-densed into a diagram. Typical symbols are shown in Figure 7.1, while Figure 7.2 illustrates a family whose eldest son, aged fourteen and the subject of a social enquiry report, has been brought up mainly by his mother, now widowed. The boy has a brother aged ten and a sister aged eight. Prior to their father dying in 1987, the children's parents were separated. Maternal grandfather died before the grandchil-dren were born, though his divorced wife, the maternal grandmother, is still alive.

Burnham (1986) gives more examples of less easy to draw family trees, such as those with multiple relationships, step-relationships and transitory contacts. Genograms can become a useful talking point for families who, while they are helping the worker to complete them, begin to uncover their family's unwritten rules, myths, secrets and taboos. For instance, my family rarely spoke about one uncle and we children assumed the worst; we discovered recently that this uncle's 'secret' is that he can neither read nor write. This map of family relationships can reveal too how patterns might get repeated across generations. Thus, the family represented in Figure 7.2 had martial breakdown, death and children reared single-handedly by their mother as repetitive themes.

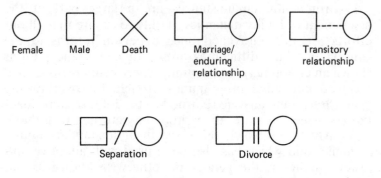

Female   Male   Death   Marriage/   Transitory
                           enduring   relationship
                           relationship

Separation   Divorce

Figure 7.1 *Genogram symbols*

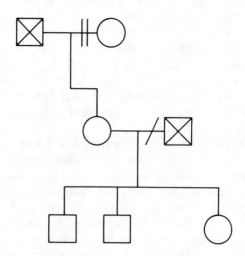

Figure 7.2 *Illustrative genogram*

If we view the family as a small organisation (but with a shared history and future), then we may see that it has a hierarchy, communication systems, values, controls, decision making, conflict resolution, norms of behaviour and ways of coping with change. Just like an organisation, a family has an invisible set of rules for how people interact with each other and how homeostasis (stability) is maintained. In order to protect themselves families develop ways of managing interactions between themselves and with outsiders. Sometimes, as we have said, these sequences and habits get in the way of moving on – they do not mean that the family is ignorant or rigid; indeed, none of us is prepared to accept change unless we know the advantages and disadvantages of this. What used to be termed 'resistance to change' has fortunately been rethought recently (Carpenter and Treacher, 1989) and I shall therefore look at some of the latest developments later in the chapter. Likewise, there has been criticism of the notion of 'circular causality', the idea that behaviour does not have a simple, linear cause; for instance, in wife battering a 'systemic' analysis would hesitate to look for a 'cause' or someone to blame. Again we shall return to this in a moment.

Possibly, it is only when we join an organisation that we learn how it really works. The same is true of families. Only if we achieve an alliance (throughout the process, not just at the beginning) together with an attitude that they are 'okay', will we ever have any inkling of what is going on.

This is not the same as saying that we approve of everything they do; in fact, as Dale and his colleagues at the NSPCC propose (Dale *et al.*, 1986), professionals can act dangerously if they trust the family too much or have too much optimism that things will improve. What it does mean is that taking time to listen to every member's point of view, being courteous, not taking sides and not confronting them with what you see as the 'truth' of their difficulties is more likely to encourage discussion and sharing in which the worker is free to engage and disengage when the need arises. Further aspects of the therapeutic alliance will be signalled when we look at techniques of practice.

Finally, to improve the assessment of family dynamics, some writers have devised assessment scales; these aim to help practitioners objectively evaluate strengths and risks, for instance with incestuous families (Orten and Rich, 1988). The format focuses on behavioural rather than psychodynamic factors such that realistic plans may be formulated. So that, with father–daughter incest, if the parent denies the abuse, blames the victim and is mainly concerned about the consequences for self these are negative indications for the assessment of future risk. Though such instruments are not infallible they may prevent working harder and harder to get families to care for their children when, at times, they may be telling us that they are unable to do so.

Four theoretical viewpoints in family therapy

Based on an understanding of family dynamics, there are a range of interventions, spanning psychoanalytic to behavioural approaches, available to the worker. We shall examine the central tenets of four of these; psychoanalytic, structural, strategic and behavioural. All of them, in recent times, have been used in combination with systems ideas, previously outlined.

1. *Psychoanalytic* models (see Box *et al.*, 1981) emphasise historical factors, uncovering unresolved conflicts from the past which continue to attach themselves to individual members of the family and their current situation. Names of therapists associated with this approach include Nathan Ackerman, Robin Skynner and Christopher Dare. The latter, interviewing a family whose son stole his mother's tights and lipsticks whenever she went into hospital, explored the mother's relationship with her father in order to help the whole family gain insight into transgenerational family patterns.

The role of the therapist is to make interpretations of individual and family patterns and focus on how members feel about each other. In addition, there is an attempt to reduce interlocking pathologies; examples of these are when children are drawn in to act as 'marital distance regulators' (Byng-Hall and Campbell, 1981) or when symptoms such as children soiling are part of projected marital conflicts (Mainprice, 1974). Some of the tools used include the genogram and sculpting (using a tableau vivant to express emotional ties). With one family whose teenage son had taken on his father's role following divorce, a sculpt showed the family how little space was left for father to fit in again, once the spouses agreed to remarry.

2. *Structural* models 'start where the family is', centring on present transactions, though the influence of what habits and role assignments have been learned earlier may be part of the assessment. People associated with this approach include Salavadore Minuchin, and in the UK, Andy Treacher and John Carpenter. Change in the way that a family's members deal with each other 'here-and-now', in the session, is the focus of the change effort. The worker joins the system to see how it works; to avoid being unable to withdraw from time to time, strategies have been devised to prevent getting too drawn in. These might be having a co-worker in the room or linked by audio/video facilities; physically withdrawing at intervals helps as does leaving fairly long intervals of two or three weeks between interviews. The goal is to restructure the family's organisation so as to change unhelpful patterns of relating to one another. For instance, films produced showing Minuchin working with families show him asking a child who is carrying parental responsibility to keep out of problem solving while an overlooked parental figure tries on this role; one child I saw with a co-worker was closer to her mother because her father was either pushed out or pulled himself out of family transactions – the direction given was for mother to encourage father there and then to talk with his daughter for a time. Some of the specific techniques include working with different sets of subsystems; changing boundaries, e.g. by seating arrangements or task-setting as above; 'tracking' which approves of family functioning by mirroring it, commenting on it and sharing information about one's own family; encouraging people to interact and then stage-

directing them to try a different pattern in the session and at home.

3. *Strategic* models keep the time focus on the present. The hypothesis is that current problems or symptoms are being maintained by ongoing, repetitive sequences of interaction between family members. Rather than historical events or unconscious conflicts determining behaviour, particular family 'truths', solutions to problems, communication mechanisms and mental constructs are given as explanations for the persistence of difficulties. There is nothing inherently 'wrong' with the family; in their efforts to sort out a solution, they have redoubled their efforts producing a 'more of the same' rut. Theorists associated with this viewpoint are Jay Haley, Mara Selvini-Palazzoli and Milton Erickson. Usually, the methods of helping are active, time-limited, focused on the attempted solution, planned ahead of the session and directed at problem solving. This might involve a team approach, using techniques such as circular questioning (mentioned in Chapter 1), neutrality and delivery of a prescription, given at the end of a session, on how the family should proceed. Because some of these prescriptions are paradoxical in nature (for instance, suggesting no change in the family in order to get them out of keep trying more of the same) some of the techniques have been decried as manipulative and disrespectful.

Families were thought to resist change because the presenting problem was needed by them to serve a function in their system. Thus, a family with a member suffering from schizophrenic illness might unknowingly resist attempts at change, fearing that the removal of the disorder in one person could unbalance family homeostasis. In other words, another relationship sequence more feared might be triggered by the change. In one family, a twelve-year-old girl had become 'paralysed' for some time, despite no organic cause being found. All kinds of systems had been found by the family to cope with this symptom (what are known as 'redundant' behaviour sequences): these might be viewed as metaphors for the family saying that they could not move on through their life cycle; interventions might encompass 'reframing', i.e. implying that this was a positive solution, e.g. in bringing them closer together or giving directives that the chronic problem continue and get worse.

Workers in this way are using the family's language – to the above family the paralysis might not be talked of as an illogical feature of family life. However, as I commented earlier, some of the theories about resistance are being rethought. In their clear text, which offers an alternative to the somewhat adversarial strategic approaches, Carpenter and Treacher (1989) note that families who come to our agencies do so because of change, either one that has taken place or is in prospect. What families need is a worker who *expects* change, seeing it not only as possible, but inevitable. Noting strengths and family cooperation is preferred to noting the pathology of resistance. Indeed, we ourselves may be what is producing the resistance, failing to match what the family need with what we have to offer.

4. *Behavioural* models again emphasise what is happening in the present, focusing on interpersonal/environmental factors which are 'rewarding', i.e. maintaining behaviour patterns. Generally, marital therapists, working with the relationship of a couple, rather than on individual 'failings', favour the methods; thus couples are taught to improve their communication skills, sexual satisfaction, assertiveness and negotiation skills, practising in-between interviews with homework tasks. Behaviour might be viewed as faulty learning or copying from one's own parents. Directing a couple to try out different behaviours in the session itself is common, with the worker operating as a trainer, model or contract negotiator. Therapists such as John Gottman (see Gottman *et al.*, 1977), R. Liberman and Michael Crowe are usually associated with this viewpoint. The latter therapist, like others, is beginning to integrate common elements from the four 'schools' of thought so that he uses structural and strategic techniques to extend his behavioural marital therapy.

Before outlining ways of beginning to work with families, I would like to briefly pursue a few of the criticisms of the concept of circular causality, alluded to earlier. Family therapists who base their practice on systemic thinking suggest that while some events can be described in a linear, cause and effect way (that A causes B which has no feedback effect on A), this does not account for complex human interactions. To take one situation; can it be said that a husband drinks because his wife gets depressed without considering that both are involved in the sequence? Another valid explanation could be that his drinking causes the depression. Seeing events in this 'whole' or systems way reveals that each person is part of a circular system of action and reaction which can begin and end at any point and therefore there is little point in asking, 'Who started it?' However, one big problem with this circular view of events, as I cautioned in the first edition of this book, is that it ignores the unequal distribution of power. Where power is an obvious factor, such as the use of violence in marriage against women in the main, then this idea of complementarity, that behaviours fit together, is questionable (see e.g. Perelberg and Miller, 1990).

A feminist critique of family therapy's systems framework might highlight:

(a)   That it preserves conventional male and female relationships.

(b)   How women clients are told what to do to be 'good wives and mothers', mirroring society's expectations.

(c)   Its preoccupation with the nuclear and immediate family, ignoring the fact that many women get a lot of emotional support from other women.

(d)   The family as a primary arena where women suffer injustice because of their sex (which is why so many institutions are required to ensure its continued existence).

(e)   The functional assumption that achieving balance in the family system is a common goal for each individual; whereas, say for the battered woman, there is inherent conflict when one person has more power than another.

(f)   The pathologising of women's emotions or the labelling of someone as 'unfeminine' who does not enjoy child-rearing or housework.

(g)   The minutiae of technique which, as O'Brian (1990) points out in relation to racism, confines work to the family system rather than its links to the social structure.

As Carpenter and Treacher (1989) comment, in every organisation there are winners and losers; the same is true of families and marriages where, in general, it is usually the loser who seeks help to restore their position. The winner has the least to gain by seeking help and is therefore a reluctant customer. Nevertheless, some writers have observed that it is possible to be a family therapist and a feminist (Pilalis and Anderton, 1986). Indeed, it could be an ideal position from which to challenge a family's assumptions and routines. Just as those in community work have helped to raise consciousness, social workers in family situations and in marital work, without imposing their values, might address the issue of power, using their advocacy, negotiation and education skills. Otherwise, as Hanmer and Statham (1988) predict,

> men will be making policies for predominantly women clients, while women will be responsible for carrying out these policies in monitoring and controlling the behaviour of women. (p. 103)

Beginning to work with families

Gorell Barnes (1984) and Burnham (1986) provide us with examples of 'selling lines' and letters to attract families so that we have people to work with! However, it is well known that when the concrete needs of families are met in the initial stages of helping, it is more likely that they will stay with us to carry on helping them to solve their other difficulties. So, practical needs may have to be dealt with first. Similarly,

O'Brian (1990) offers the following guidelines for planning work with black families:

– be clear about who is asking for your involvement; if it is an agency, what do the family feel about this?
– is the referral discriminatory, e.g. have the services failed the family? (He gives an example of a school who referred a pupil because 'West Indian parents are not interested in education'.)
– if the above is the case, should you deal with the referring system first? (They could be informed that usually parents are concerned and if need be invited to the first meeting, held in the school.)
– beware cultural stereotyping oneself.
– should direct work with the family be done by someone who shares their experience of racism?

With all referrals, as was stated in Chapter 1 on assessment, the referring person is a key figure and, occasionally, is the problem.

Before the first meeting with the family it will be necessary to explain why the whole family need to be involved, saying, for instance, 'If there's a problem in the family it's bound to affect everyone' or 'It helps to get everyone's ideas about what could help'. Even then, as we have seen, families who have a history of being on 'the books' of a variety of agencies naturally resent intrusion and what they see as victimisation by professionals. Strategies for engaging families with many problems might start by acknowledging their loyalty to each other and how difficult their problems must be to cope with. Underlying dilemmas can be confronted too, how raising some issues is hard on them but yet they may have tried to change without success. Where numerous organisations are involved, the use of a network meeting to prevent overlap and duplication can reduce pressure on the family, as can home visits when families are short of money.

Families who have received a lot of help are sometimes isolated – they also may need connecting to a support network of friends, relatives and sympathetic neighbours. It is vital to respect people and their cultural values, confirming too that they are still in charge of any changes which they choose to make. Many family therapists help the group to weigh the pros and cons of change, slowing down hasty decisions, confirming the family's underlying need for stability.

Haley (1976) helpfully divides the interview into four stages; a social stage, problem stage, interaction stage and ending stage. Taking each in turn, the *social stage* is worth taking time over. Being courteous, getting to know everyone, asking them to sit where they wish if it is away from their home, introducing oneself, carefully trying to remember everyone's name and interests, checking if anyone is missing, noting the mood and how they deal with you and each other are some starting points. When someone is absent this could be a sign of non-cooperation; on the other hand, there may be genuine practical problems or, as I found working with an adolescent, he sometimes wanted to be seen without his parents and this was respected. Home visits can be less stigmatising and less threatening for the family, but it may mean the worker being active in asking for a barking dog to be removed or a television set switched off. Preventing a headlong discussion of the problem is necessary as this can result in certain members being neglected. Clarify what you know of their situation and why you wanted them all to be there.

The *problem stage* starts by asking what is the problem or how you can help or what changes they want. Listen to everyone's views without making interpretations, offering advice or trying to get them to see the problem your way. Find out the detail of who does what to whom and how the problem affects individuals, using circular questioning when appropriate. It may *not* be appropriate when the worker and the clients are from different ethnic backgrounds: for example; saying that everyone is different, allowing children to have a voice, objecting to older children looking after younger ones and so on could lead to disagreements (Liverpool, 1986). A therapeutic alliance relies on us checking our attitudes and assumptions and increasing our knowledge of other cultures (see Lau, 1984). Still, as O'Brian (1990) reminds us,

152   *Social Work Practice*

Black parents do mistreat their children. Elderly black people are
not always cared for by their families. Black women are subjected to
domestic violence. (p. 8)

In the *interaction stage* involve everyone with each other;
often this happens anyway as members begin to talk to one
another. This is probably how they solve their problems so
you may be less active, watching the speakers and the
listeners, only directing when the focus on problem solving
appears to drift.

Bearing in mind differences in culture mentioned above,
you may ask certain members to talk to one another rather
than you keep the attention on their suggestions and solutions. You have to strive to maintain an alliance with the family, supporting strengths, perhaps putting yourself in the one-
down position but being persistent, recognising their fears
and sometimes addressing these. The family may try to deter
you with the dog or the television, or by denying the
problem, blaming others or drawing you into their viewpoint, showing how helpless they are: when the time is right,
you can talk generally about taking change slowly and
aiming for very limited goals of their choosing so as to
engage them and take their fears seriously.

The *ending stage* should see some agreement on a simple
goal, arrangements for future meetings, any tasks to be
achieved in-between and time limits sorted out. With some
families, it may have been the only planned meeting with the
whole group; where families turn down family therapy as an
approach, they may accept just one meeting of this kind for
assessment purposes. Who is to attend in the future may be
planned, though working hardest with the least committed
person can sometimes get them to come back.

Case example

Sue, thirteen, had not been to school for a year. The school
social worker had never seen her as Sue refused to come
downstairs during home visits. A psychiatric assessment was
planned, but the family, which included three older sisters

who had all left home, agreed instead to work as a group. A male colleague from an area social services team and myself saw them at home in the evenings on four occasions. Prior to contact, we hypothesised from their life-cycle stage and their family tree that Sue might be struggling with adolescent challenges while her parents faced re-forming as a couple, preparing for the prospect of their last child leaving home.

We knew from the education social worker that father was a long-distance lorry driver, who had never been inter-viewed, and that mother and daughter were very close. There was some suggestion of marital violence throughout the marriage, plus some strict disciplining of the three other sisters. We wondered if the women needed to ally them-selves against father's physical power; in family therapy terms, this would cross hierarchical and generational bound-aries. Also, when men are temporarily absent from the family and return at intervals from their jobs, this increases strain on the couple who have to continually re-negotiate space, decision making and roles.

On each visit, timed to coincide with father's trips home, we often had to wait for him to arrive. Though there was some pressure to begin without him we resisted this because otherwise this would have been no different from previous problem solving which had not produced change. We had to show that we were 'with them' but at the same time objectively trying to help them sort out Sue's non-attendance at school. So, we drank tea and chatted about the older sisters' jobs, mother's part-time work as a cleaner which she enjoyed and which gave her some financial independence.

We started the 'formal' business once father arrived; he was a largely built man, quite intimidating to look at but my colleague and I treated him as if he were cooperative, asking him to plug in our audiotape which he happily complied with. (The reason for this and returning the tapes to the family on completion had been discussed.) Sometimes, just as in network assemblies, the mere bringing together of a whole family is powerful enough to unblock communications or prevent them being diverted through something or someone else. Thus it was with this family; although Sue never spoke, she listened intently as the women bravely confronted her father's over-zealous disciplining. He confessed he was ashamed of once having tipped one of them out of bed and looked astonished when his wife said that she intended leaving him once Sue had left school. She planned to get a full-time job and establish her independence. Sue had never been hit by her father; she looked young and boyish with jeans and a short haircut, but kept her head bowed throughout most of our meetings. We wondered if mother would take Sue with her when she left and she said that she had not decided. We addressed what seemed to be connected themes of growing up and leaving home, using our co-therapy relationship to model problem solving and respect for each other's views. Tentatively we suggested, 'Perhaps Sue is sacrificing her growing up to save the family from splitting up?'

Using circular questioning, we revealed different viewpoints, introducing new information about how each third party saw relationships in the family, in regard to the specific problem but also, because the family's reality was that marital conflict was an issue, we asked, 'When your mother rows with your father what does Sue do?' and, 'When your mother leaves home, who will be most and who will be least upset?'.

In many ways, we provided a channel for the family talking about something which had been simmering for some time but which all were afraid to confront. Since the older girls had ideas about growing up and managing school we decided to draw on their expertise. Working with the sibling subsystem on their own for a time in the front room, we set tasks for the older sisters to confide in Sue what their teenage years had been like. Their parents agreed with us that none of us would enquire about these get-togethers. After six weeks, during which the sisters met each other for these talks, which all enjoyed, Sue returned to school where she subsequently did extremely well. The married couple believed that they would carry on sorting out their plans for their relationship; neither wanted help with this and, some time later, they are still married.

Working with couples

Prior to drawing up a framework for this approach I want to add a few additional comments on marital or couples work. While the theoretical viewpoints remain the same, in that there are psychoanalytic, structural, strategic and behavioural forms of work, usually based on systems thinking, other points are important to mention. One is that social work students and practitioners seem to be reluctant to engage in marital work. Maybe it is 'too close to home'; most of us have experienced marriage at close quarters and some have experienced the trauma of marital breakdown. The agencies, outside of specialist ones like Relate, also appear to sustain this defence against working with anxiety provoking, intimate material, preferring to work with one of the couple and then mainly in terms of resource giving.

Having decided to work with marital difficulties, James and Wilson (1986) give a useful breakdown of how to proceed; when to work with the marital system or one partner, whether the goal is enriching the relationship or freeing from it. These authors also have a useful chapter in their book on working with couples from minority ethnic groups, again recommending that we look beyond cultural stereotypes of, for instance, the subordination of South Asian women or the issue of arranged marriages.

What one might find in the initial assessment of a couple whose relationship is fundamentally stable is that they have sought help with a transitional crisis: often expectations of marriage are too high and they are unaware that there is no marriage without conflict. Spouses sometimes project the unwanted part of themselves on to the other so that there is a great deal of blaming and attempts to make the social worker an ally of one partner. However, referrals, especially to statutory agencies, often come in the guise of problems with parental roles, attacks from the family of origin, continual threats of separation and eviction which stem from ambivalent marital bonds (see Mattinson and Sinclair, 1979). These are marriages characterised by instability, where there is difficulty in trusting each other and making attachments, related to a deep-seated longing for love and security. Because of this, there may be a lot of work to be done with the individuals on their own as well as on their relationship.

Incidentally although therapists prefer to work conjointly (with both partners) there is no objection to seeing only one. Carpenter and Treacher (1989) place an empty chair in the room and say something like, 'If John were here what would he say?', as well as giving (usually a woman) support to get the other person to accept help.

Where problems are sexual ones, generally, as we have seen, behavioural methods are preferred, although a deeper understanding may be required if these have little effect. For instance, some couples dread differentiation; they keep negative feelings and differences out of their marriage, thereby frustrating adult sexual roles. (Books by the Institute of Marital Studies, e.g. *The Marital Relationship as a Focus for Casework* are valuable in exploring psychodynamic factors in marriage.) Many of the underlying problems for couples, heterosexual or otherwise, are about intimacy and distance, sameness and difference or how each person gets their needs met, 'how often each can be allowed to be the baby' (Clulow and Mattinson, 1989, p.56).

Framework for understanding family and couples' work

Theoretical base is systems theory used in combination with psychodynamic, structural, strategic and behavioural ideas. Important concepts include the question of causality, boundaries, hierarchy, homeostasis and interactions inside the family and with the suprasystem, i.e. external systems.

Problems are those of family transactions; family problem-solving patterns and communications which become blocked, distorted or displaced through one member. Myths, secrets and taboos carried over from previous generations might also hinder problem solving. A number of problems arise as a response to life-cycle transitions when there is a need to flexibly adapt and re-align relationships. Some solutions could become the problem.

Goals are minimal, often aimed at changing overt behaviour, though some methods aim at insight as well. The family are helped to choose limited, specific goals, usually within a brief time frame. Workers aim to 'join' the family or couple, inasmuch as they offer support while attempts are made at restructuring relationship patterns and behavioural sequences.

The client's role. In this approach, the couple or the family is the client. They may also be the target for change and the team which works alongside the therapeutic team to change transactional patterns within or outside their system.

The worker's role. There may be two workers as co-therapists or a therapeutic team who hypothesise how the system of family transactions relate to the problem presented. Work with external systems could be just as important, especially when numerous agencies are involved who unwittingly mirror family dynamics. It is vital to sustain the couple's or the family's attempt at problem solving; not take sides or blame; not perpetuate power inequalities but to raise awareness of these and to offer a positive redefinition of their difficulties to help those who have become stuck trying 'more of the same'.

Techniques are numerous. This is why caution is advised against being bewitched by technique at the expense of helping the family in an authentic, non-adversarial way. Joining and restructuring operations include tracking communications and themes about family life (sticking to detail helps; mundane themes often reveal the typical ways in which people manage each other); intensity around the specific problem might be necessary in order to break out of 'redundant' problem-solving routines; observation is as important as listening, so that process and content, how the family behave and what is said, are clues to helping, and being careful not to undermine family competence but to confirm their strengths. Other methods involve use of the family tree and genogram; creating physical space and shifting relationship boundaries; setting tasks; taking time out of the interview to check with colleagues what is happening, or using 'live' supervision with the supervisor in the room to ensure effectiveness and objectivity. More

'advanced' techniques, aimed at exceptionally chronic difficulties, might be the use of paradoxical prescriptions (advis-
ing no change) and the (possibly gifted) use of metaphor,
stories and anecdotes. Self-disclosure, in a self-aware
worker, can be used on occasion to talk about one's own
family life.

8

Working with Groups

Every method that we have discussed so far you will find can be used when working with groups. Much of the early literature on groupwork arose from group analytic methods. There is growing interest in the effectiveness of cognitive therapy with groups, while some writers view family therapy as groupwork (Zastrow, 1985). However, because family therapy uses such different methods, despite many concepts being the same, I prefer not to talk of it as groupwork. Despite the specialism of community work lying outside the scope of this book (see Twelvetrees, 1991), many such workers depend on groupwork as a major form of intervention. In the same way, what follows may be of interest to staff teams intent on developing community social work: I know that agencies in the north-east are creatively using groupwork to extend the networks of carers and service users, to promote self-directed groups and to develop new resources such as parent and toddler groups.

Taking the definition of a group as a collection of people who spend some time together, who see themselves as members and who are identified by outsiders as members of a group (Preston-Shoot, 1987) this chapter introduces some of the types and purposes of groups. It comments on the tasks for the worker, discusses how to handle particular difficulties and recommends literature which practice teachers and students tell me is most accessible and which they like. The case example is of group assertiveness training.

159

Types and purposes of groups

It is an interesting exercise to list the number of groups of which you are or have been a member. These experiences, though, do not necessarily help us to analyse what is going on unless we have studied group dynamics. The leadership of groups is yet a further skill which may only be learned by doing. It helps, however, to understand that group aims usually prescribe the type and methods to use. Different purposes are those broadly categorised by Papell and Rothman (1966) – remedial, reciprocal and social goals models. In detail, Preston-Shoot (1987) distinguishes social or recreational groups; group psychotherapy; group counselling; educational groups; social treatment groups (e.g. Intermediate Treatment); discussion groups; self-help groups; social action groups (e.g. welfare rights), and self-directed groups (e.g. campaigning or other objectives decided by the members).

The reason why groups fail to 'get going' might be related to how they are formed, composed and led, but also a failure to be clear about purposes. While during its lifetime a group may change its purposes, for instance from discussion to campaigning, unless it is openly stated at the outset what the purposes are, groups can 'lose their way' and become very puzzling for their members. One group, supposedly a recreational one for single parent mothers, had a hidden agenda aimed at getting the women to improve their parenting skills. So, it was doomed from the start. Whitaker (1975) shows how a group could be retrieved by bearing in mind four issues:

1. Success is more likely if other people in the agency support the group purpose and procedures. Sabotage is also less likely.
2. A group is more likely to be effective if a consensus can be established within the group about aims and methods.
3. Structural factors such as size, duration, composition, constancy of membership and ratio of staff to members influence effectiveness.

4. A group which has lost its purpose should be reconstituted with a different mandate or terminated.

The only reason for using groupwork as opposed to any other practice method is that it is the best way of helping the people concerned, not because the workers want to try it. Indeed, groups have their disadvantages, not least that some individuals are frightened of them. Having experienced tyranny in one group to which I belonged, I would certainly hesitate to include anyone whose self-esteem was at a low ebb. On the other hand, groups provide what Yalom (1970) terms 'curative factors' not available through individual approaches. They can be a source of power for clients pressing for social change; mutual support, exchange of information and motivating hope also stem from group processes. Groups offer the opportunity to learn and test interpersonal and other social skills; they offer a sense of belonging and 'being in the same boat' which is reassuring. There is scope to use the leader or other members as role models and to get feedback about coping attempts. Perhaps, most significantly, there is a chance to help as well as be helped.

Planning the group

Having decided on the type and broad aims of the group, a major task is planning and preparation. Questions to be answered comprise:

– *Who*? The composition of a group may already be determined, such as those in hospital wards, residential and day centres and neighbourhoods. Where the group can be formed, an ideal balance suggested by Redl (1951) is, 'homogeneous enough to ensure stability and heterogeneous to ensure vitality'. Racial homogeneity might be necessary where this is preferred by minority ethnic groups (see Sheik, 1986); similarly, sameness of gender may best meet the purposes of the group (see Reed and Garvin, 1983). But, overall, perhaps the best guide is commonality of needs.

– *How many*? The question of group size depends on the aims of the group, but usually there needs to be more than three and less than fourteen people, what Brown (1986) suggests is 'large enough for stimulation, small enough for participation and recognition'.

– *How long*? Open-ended or time-limited, this question also needs to incorporate a decision whether or not to have open or closed membership. (In hospital social work I found there was little choice, as patients and staff on shift systems came and went.) The length of each session needs to be considered too, for instance work with children or elderly people who are frail (see Cornish, 1983) requires short sessions with rest breaks.

– *Which methods*? The methods must suit the members, skills of the leader(s) and the stated aims. It may be that it is only when the group has met that final decisions can be taken. Then there are a variety of games, discussions, activities, experiential exercises and entertainments available (the *Annual Handbook for Group Fcilitators* is a worthwhile source). Boyce and Anderson (1990) use drama therapy, video and written exercises in their group-work with adolescent girls who have been sexually abused; Walker (1978) did not have specific aims in her work with emotionally starved women clients in the Family Service Unit, and so her methods were essentially parenting and nurturing ones.

– *What resources*? There are a number of practical issues to be addressed such as is there a meeting place; is transport available if necessary; will refreshments be provided; what equipment is needed and so on? Furthermore, the agency may want a breakdown of costs in terms of time spent, staffing by one leader or two, if an outside consultant is to be used, what recording systems will be used and if workers in the whole team can make referrals, for instance from their current workloads.

Stages of group development and the worker's tasks

Groups evolve through stages when their behaviour, the leader's interventions and the accomplishment of tasks or activities are affected. Following individual 'screening' (for client and worker!) you have to be confident that you can follow the energy of the group through trust, openness, interdependence and finally independence. At different stages, the worker has to be central, pivotal, peripheral and central once again. Accordingly, the worker is in tune with the stages of group development known as forming, storming, norming, performing and adjourning (Tuckman and Jensen, 1977).

Other groupwork theorists name these stages differently, but all agree the phenomena to be observed at each: Yalom (1970) describes orientation, conflict then cohesiveness; Schutz (1966) outlined cycles when the group is concerned with inclusion, control and affection, while Whitaker (1985) talks about formative, established and termination phases.

Quickly, in the forming stages, members move from orientation and exploration, in which there is parallel communication aimed at the worker, to more communications with each other. The group and the worker is tested to see if trust can be established. The tasks for the practitioner are to help people to get involved, to link people and their common concerns and to encourage the development of a group bond. When any of us join a group we want to know if the sacrifice of our individual wants will be compensated for by joining the group so the worker takes any opportunity to point out how they, sharing similar interests and problems, are in a position to understand and thereby help one another. To summarise the skills and tasks of the leader in the early meetings:

– give a short presentation of yourself
– ask members to do the same
– review information given to members prior to joining
– amend any aims and agreements
– acknowledge initial uncertainties
– get each person to say what they hope to get out of the group
– summarise issues as presented
– establish norms for listening and accepting
– facilitate interaction, 'Does anybody else feel the same?'

– play the absent member role, putting into wor
  people may want to say but are not yet ready to
– show concern for each individual
– balance answering questions with 'Does anyone els
  the answer to that?' (Northen, 1969; Heap, 1985).

During the storming stage, subgroups and pairing ma
formed (later, these relationships extend to inclu
whole group). It is a stage characterised by the replacement
of 'Do I belong?' with, 'Do I have any influence?'. Struggles
for power and control underlie communications and there is
a tendency for members to polarise around certain issues.
Further exploring and testing takes place: the group is quite
fragile and may not continue if the leadership does not
provide enough security while individuals query if they are
going to get what they came for. This stage can be draining.
Some skills and tasks are:

– keep calm in the face of member–member, member–
  leader conflicts
– do not retaliate when your authority is challenged; it may
  stem from ambivalence about membership or a transference reaction.
– model acceptance and openly recognise that people are
  different
– do not pick out isolated or difficult members for attention
– try to pace and time when to facilitate and when to be
  quiet
– begin to release responsibilities to the membership

The norming stage indicates that group cohesion is established; intimate and personal opinions may be expressed by
members to each other. People start to look for 'affection',
i.e. signs that they are accepted by the wider circle. Cooperation, sharing information and decision making by consensus promote synergistic (the extra power of combined action) outcomes. People identify with the group and its
future: a 'we' feeling develops, a growing *ésprit de corps*. A
norm of high attendance, ritual ownership of seats and some
exclusivity is likely to make it difficult for new members to
join. A lack of conformity to group norms can lead to

scapegoating or group pressure to conform. New leadership from within the group may result in altering basic group norms. For the worker, the tasks are to:

– let people help each other by stepping out of a directing role into a listening, following one
– be pivotal when observing and commenting on what seems to be happening, asking the group what their perceptions are as well as offering ideas of your own
– be more aware of process as well as content; it helps to ask oneself (and perhaps the group), 'What is going on here? What is this issue really all about?' in order to help people to express feelings and challenge comments.

When performing occurs, this means that the group has developed a culture of acting together to solve problems: it is no longer the leader's group, rather the worker becomes peripheral as the members perceive that 'This is our group'. Individual and group goals are tackled, meaning that members model coping mechanisms and values for each other. A high status or charismatic member may further enhance a group's willingness to let individuals 'try on' different roles, thus preparing for eventual differentiation and independence from the group. One member in a group I ran had always been relied on as the 'competent and responsible' one: at this stage he acted as a facilitator for the rest by bravely pointing out that sometimes he did not feel confident and would prefer sometimes to take a break from feeling responsible. The worker:

– observes how the group handle each other and the tasks
– gives ideas when these are sought
– shows interest and expresses praise and appreciation of efforts
– continues to model in relation to confidence, attitudes and problem solving

The ending or adjourning stage usually follows the achievement of the task and requires disengagement from relationships. All groups have to end sometime otherwise they risk stagnation or low productivity. Imposed time limits can prevent the worker from hanging on to a group merely because he or she feels guilty or uncertain about 'letting go'. There will be a sense of loss and maybe rejection but also of achievement. The worker, more active again, can:

- set goals for the time left in partnership with the group
- review experiences, emphasising gains as well as feelings of loss
- reinforce interests outside the group
- help the group to return to the planning stage if they want to continue but with some other purpose
- evaluate the sessions and ask for feedback.

Handling difficulties in groups

Describing group development through the above phases might suggest that all is straightforward and predictable when, in reality, stages only represent tendencies from which any group can veer. Furthermore, there is a great deal of what Heap (1985) calls 'latent' communication in groups which demands greater diagnostic understanding and group-work skill. Often, there are recurring themes, for instance, when a group seems preoccupied with a particular, apparently irrelevant topic. This might be mistakenly ignored instead of associated with something people cannot talk about directly. Literature in groupwork refers to this as a common group tension or focal conflict. Heap (1985) gives an example of a group of prospective adoptive parents, who, while waiting for a child, were brought together for general discussions about child development and adoptive experiences. One day, the worker found the group heatedly discussing legislation giving shopkeepers the right to open and close when they chose. The group was angry and resentful at being at the whims of possessors of valued goods. An indirect communication was the group's anger with the adoption agency's powerful witholding of children from them. Recognising the deeper meaning of content and managing the processes around focal conflicts takes sensitivity and advanced skills.

Beyond symbolic communication difficulties, workers fantasise about the possibility that a group will simply take no notice of the leader or that strong emotions will result in chaos and damaged individuals. Books which suggest techniques, such as that by Corey *et al.* (1982) can inspire some confidence until more experience is gained. But even experienced workers are anxious when a group member is isolated, scapegoated, speaks too much or too little. Generally, many of these difficulties can be put back to the group for their resolution; otherwise individual counselling might help or it may be that the behaviour is needed by the group for some reason and should be explored.

In addressing the scapegoat phenomenon, for instance, Shulman (1979) suggests that the worker first observe the pattern, tunes into her/his own feelings about this, avoids siding with or against the scapegoat and asks the group to comment on what is happening. Then, if the scapegoat does not need protection or mediation, the worker attempts to reduce guilt, fear or whatever feelings the group is suppressing and projecting on to one member by talking about such feelings in a general way. For example, in student groups one person may be aggressive and outspoken; the rest hide their feelings so as not to be different or unpopular. It is possible to point out that what the outspoken student is saying is felt by a lot of people even though they may not admit it. Then one can go on to reflect on how social workers may fear conflict and yet it is an issue every day in practice; having the courage to confront it is what matters.

If the leader does not handle the monopoliser in the group, Yalom (1970) warns that members will start to be absent or explode! The problem with allowing someone to dominate a group is that this stops others with useful things to say from contributing. So intervention has to take place early on to prevent group structure hardening and while the leader still has patience. For example, in a group of carers, one man went on at length about his experience. As this was the first meeting, he might have overwhelmed other participants with his knowledge and so, having thanked him for prompting the group to explore a range of ideas, the worker indicated clearly that she would like to hear everyone's point

of view. Stimulating silent members counteracts monopo-
lisers as well as making the group structure a more functional one. If a person stays silent, some groups resent this
believing that the person is quietly judging them or not
sharing. Teasing silent members or saying 'We haven't heard
from you, Mrs Smith' is not helpful, whereas something like,
'I remember you said something about this once, Mrs Smith.
Could you remind us about your suggestion as I think it
would help'. Conveying an interest in hearing from people
and modelling respect can also be done non-verbally with a
touch, gesture or eye contact – swivelling one's eyes around
a student group will usually catch a reticent person who
might speak if encouraged with a nod.

Obviously, there cannot be prescriptions for handling all
the problems that arise, but Whitaker's book (1985) details
usable interventions for the newly-fledged and the experienced practitioner.

Just a few final words on recording group sessions and the
use of co-leading are needed before we proceed to the case
example. As I stated in the Introduction, with the emphasis
on economy, efficiency and effectiveness, we have to find
time-saving methods of doing both. In relation to recording,
some groupworkers keep a register showing standard information such as date; session number; members and leaders
present/absent; plan for the session; diagram of seating
arrangements; what happened (i.e. content and process); an
evaluation of what went well and what did not (Brown,
1986). Others draw a series of circles representing each
member: the circles are divided into three portions indicat-
ing the beginning, middle and end of the session, noting
atmosphere, influence, participation, tasks and decision
making at each time stage in the 'interaction chronogram'.
As far as co-leading or co-facilitating goes, Preston-Shoot
(1987) devotes some of his book to this. He says that the
advantages might be evident in large groups (though not
always); for continuity when one leader is absent; when
members might get out of control or express strong emotions
such as co-work in Intensive Intermediate Treatment and
work with people who are mentally ill, and when work will
be done in subgroups. The disadvantages could be where the

co-workers hold widely differing views on goals and styles and where the sole worker already has the resources required. Planning, selecting and presenting a co-leader to the group is also analysed as is the issue of gender combinations. The value of black social workers co-working with white social workers is not explored, though having run student groups with black colleagues, this could have been oppressive had all the students been white. In this instance, two black leaders joined myself (white) in co-facilitating workshops.

Case example: assertiveness training

Assertiveness training has proved an effective practice approach in a wide variety of circumstances and settings. It is used with children bullied in school, with youngsters in drug treatment programmes, to help women in ante-natal clinics plan the kind of births they want and to help managers in the personal social services to become confident in their task. It is used too in social work training to improve negotiation and other interpersonal skills. Increasingly, I have been using it to help workers in residential and day-care units to look after themselves and thereby better manage the stresses of the job. Although it is essentially a behavioural approach, group dynamics addressing feelings are important components in running successful sessions. A typical assertion training programme is described here.

The first meeting is devoted to getting to know everyone's names and, if there has been no chance to see people individually beforehand, a brief lecture on the philosophy and theory of assertiveness and self-esteem is given with the chance to ask questions and clarify what certain terms mean. For example, there is usually confusion around whether or not one has the 'right' to be assertive; another task is to clarify what is meant by aggressive, non-assertive and assertive behaviour. Members may suggest adjectives under each of these three headings so that aggressiveness is being bossy or invading someone's integrity; non-assertiveness is being resigned to events or avoiding confrontation, while assertiveness is being open, honest and liking oneself. Members might be asked to brainstorm a list of what rights they think that they have got, producing such items as asking for what you want, having the right to fail or be respected. Eventually the group formulate a definition of assertiveness which is agreed as standing up for basic human rights, without violating those of others, and making your behaviour match your feelings. It is added that we are all assertive at some times with some people, but that it is possible to learn to be assertive in situations at home and at work which cause stress.

In between sessions, participants may complete an assertion self-assessment table; a hierarchy of least and most anxiety provoking situations when assertiveness could be used, and a daily log of successful assertive interactions (see Langrish, 1981). These are brought along to the next meeting when someone chooses to work on an identified goal for themselves. Usually, as people share their items from the above measuring tools, they find they have a lot in common; for instance being unable to refuse requests (from 'better qualified field social workers'!), asking for supervision, receiving compliments from clients, and so on. Others might be able to handle these circumstances but are less assertive with people at home, for instance expressing affection or refusing family invitations when they have just finished an exhausting shift of duty.

The person who chooses to work on learning new skills sets up the scene for the rest so that they can see a 'slice' of the events which occur around a specific example of being non-assertive or aggressive. The whole group is engaged in helping the person achieve their stated goal, perhaps playing a part in the staging of the situation or giving feedback on how verbal, non-verbal and emotional responses be changed. In essence, the techniques resemble social skills training and cognitive-behaviour therapy detailed earlier in Chapter 6. Role playing of a particular scene, the leader encouraging the protagonist to listen to what they are telling themselves and how they feel, reveals which behaviours the person would like to try to improve. Constructive feedback from colleagues is incorporated into a replay. The leader has to make sure that the group does not fall into the familiar trap of assuming that being assertive is the same as winning, gaining power, being selfish or trying to change other people. Frequently, I find that aggression is equated with assertion in groups comprising both men and women. There is always a misunderstanding also that we have to make the other person behave differently when the goal is to look after oneself and to come out of an interaction feeling good about yourself.

To give a couple of examples of what I mean: in one role play a residential social worker overheard a colleague gossiping about her to another. First, she had to decide if she had the 'right' to say anything and feeling that she did, she confronted the gossip, pointing out how hurt she felt and how she would like it to stop. The 'audience' thought that she could have been tougher on the gossip. But all that matters is if the 'actor' themselves feels happier about the way they behaved in the replay. In another scene, a male worker was being intimidated by a bully who lived in the flat above his. In the assertiveness attempt, he was polite, friendly and seeking a compromise with the bullying neighbour; he felt satisfied with his newly learned assertion, but colleagues watching wondered if he should have taken a stronger line. Whether he should or not is not important; what was, was the worker's satisfaction that he was 'okay'. The leader has to model acceptance and deal with attempts by the group itself to impose their point of view and thereby become directly or indirectly aggressive towards each other.

Ideally, everyone should be offered the chance to work on their individual goals in this way throughout the following sessions; working on the easiest item first is usually advised. The leader teaches various techniques of assertion, sometimes using experiential and small group exercises (see Dickson (1982) whose book many of the participants buy, realizing that learning to be assertive is a life-long, not once-and-for-all business). Practising the 'middle way' is recommended to the group, that is, looking for a workable compromise if one's self respect is not at issue, rather than trying to 'win'.

Non-verbal techniques include good eye contact; confident posture such as standing or sitting comfortably without fidgeting; talking in a strong, steady voice; unclenching one's fists and not pointing one's finger. Verbal behaviour has to avoid rambling, qualifying words (such as 'maybe; only; just') plus disqualifying phrases such as, 'I'm sure this isn't important, but . . .'. Attacking phrases, such as those which begin with 'You. . .' become assertive ones when I-language, 'I feel . . .'are used instead. A formula sentence might be practised by the group, such as, 'When . . . [insert the activity], I feel . . . [insert the emotion]: I would like . . . [insert the outcome]; otherwise . . . [insert the undesirable alternative if previous statements have failed to work].'

Verbal skills include learning to say that small, but difficult word no, which as Dickson (1982) points out, is seen as uncaring for the caring, woman worker who is made to feel guilty at ever putting her needs first. (I have found with black, female managers, that even assertive behaviours are misconstrued as aggressive ones by white colleagues.) The burgeoning literature on this topic also gives the following specific behaviours to practise:

Broken Record – calm repetition of the assertive message
Fogging – accept criticism comfortably without becoming defensive
Negative enquiry – actively prompt criticism to disarm manipulation
Use silence and listen reflectively – to get others to be open with you.

Evaluation of groupwork using methods such as these indicates that individuals do acquire new skills; they feel less guilty about asking for their needs to be met; people feel more comfortable in being in groups; despite the development of group relationships not being a major goal of this type of groupwork, inevitably trust, conflict, intimacy and sadness at ending the experience permeate group process.

9

Conclusion

All social work efforts have to come to an end sometime. Termination and transfer of work may be planned or unplanned, initiated by the client or worker, mutually agreed or unilaterally decided. Closing 'cases' and ending relationships receives surprisingly little attention in the literature, though the topic of evaluation has been redis-covered by researchers and managers (see Davies and Knapp, 1988; Coulshed, 1990). Good case management, as a system and as a practice, depends on showing that we have achieved planned goals in a cost effective, accountable way. And yet Challis and Davies (1989), reporting on their work with elderly clients at home, do not lay great stress on the process of closure or arrangements made for continuing support of clients and their carers. Instead, assessment, monitoring and sustaining are held up as the main features of case management practice. Furthermore, other systems in the future might limit the social work role to identifying need then commissioning or purchasing help from other providing agencies. Whatever instruments of social welfare emerge in the coming years, social workers will continue to focus on people's well-being while relationships will still be a pervading influence. Therefore, this final chapter offers some concluding remarks about transfer and termination.

Ending social work intervention

Reasons for closure or transfer to another worker or agency are diverse. They include:

- agreed goals being achieved within a pre-set time
- clients deciding they have been helped enough
- workers leaving or clients moving from the district
- the end of statutory requirements
- agency policy on time limits
- workload management and priority systems
- resource limitations
- lack of time and pressure of work
- advice from supervisor
- influence of other agencies
- death of the client.

We saw in the chapters on crisis intervention, task-centred practice and behavioural approaches how these models were developed to allow for built-in termination. It was viewed as a positive step, a way of motivating people by focusing efforts at specified goals. Equally, family and marital therapists tell us that we should recognise when enough is enough (Carpenter and Treacher, 1989), letting families and couples get on with their lives without us. In the previous chapter, it was recommended that groupworkers and community social workers take the process of termination seriously, learning to anticipate possible reactions of denial, backsliding into earlier difficulties, reminiscing and reviewing the worth of the experience. But, unfortunately, not all methods of helping or settings for practice lend themselves to a rational model which sets goals, assesses progress and then smoothly start the process of withdrawing. For example, in a Barnardo's project to find foster families for adults with severe learning disabilities and challenging behaviour, a key worker found herself having to say goodbye to a man she had worked with intensively for nine years. He and she were devastated despite the new attachment to the foster family having been spread over a long period.

Though written some time ago, a couple of articles by Bywaters (1975) help us to understand why so many of our contacts end, not with a sense of achievement and neatness, but with feelings of loss, work not completed or not even begun. His research into social services revealed bureaucratic, theoretical and psychological drawbacks for clients and workers which affected both the decision to close or transfer as well as the process of achieving this. Coupled with the above organisational reasons for closing cases, he found that workers often felt that they could not control endings and neither were clients consulted about the decision. Social workers tended not to use the time-limited approaches; many were aiming for more extensive goals than clients were aware of, using open-ended casework methods. Practitioners often felt that they could do more or that cases should be left open until a resource such as housing became available. Moreover, feelings of guilt, uncertainty and loss affected the process of handling endings. Thus, staff felt guilty knowing that time spent with one person was time not spent with another; uncertainty about their effectiveness plus the client's ability to cope in the future impeded a positive approach to endings; feeling lost and resentful after putting in a lot of work were other reactions.

Clients and workers may experience transfer or termination of work as a type of crisis (even if the attachment has been short term) if each has invested a part of themselves. Students on placement report feelings of sadness and anxiety at 'abandoning' clients; the death of a client is especially distressing and might need reassurance that shedding tears is not unprofessional. Clients and workers may be reminded of earlier losses by the experience of closure. And yet, much in the same way that crisis prevention was possible with 'worry work' and preparation, clients and workers can anticipate endings in advance, enhancing their growth-promoting opportunities.

A good model of ending could incorporate the following:

1. A discussion in the first meeting that help will not go on for ever. Clients' feelings and perceptions of this are important and need to be sensitively handled. For instance, those in crisis might ask, 'How long will this take?' and, for some, it might be reassuring to know that help will not suddenly be withdrawn. For others, it may be a relief to know that a social worker will not always need to visit.

2. Using the experience of termination or transfer as a learning one for the client rather than a painful, separating one. In groupwork it was noted that transitions are eased when people are helped to wean away from the experience – outside relationships and activities are rewarded. Confirming the client's self-confidence and self-reliance underlines what they have gained and how they have dealt with the experience of help coming to an end.

3. Where possible employing a fixed time limit purposefully, using time itself as a therapeutic agent.

4. Giving the client certain objectives to achieve in the ending phase.

5. Beforehand, exploring a person's feelings about the end of the relationship. (Anticipate possible setbacks, which provide opportunity for worry work.) Gradual withdrawal helps such as reducing the frequency of meetings, arranging for semi-independent living accommodation, progressively leaving longer time with future carers and so on.

6. Introduce the new worker if there is to be one and talk in that meeting about the fact that the client could well feel very angry about the arrangement. After one social worker did this, the client vented much resentment but then was free to build a fresh relationship with the incoming practitioner.

7. Help the person construct a natural helping network in the community, mobilising practical resources if need be. Then do a follow-up visit.

8. Explore your own feelings; show the client that you will remember them; have confidence in their ability to manage without you but express the goodwill of the agency whose door is left open should they need to return for further help.

9. In some contexts a ritual or ceremonial ending with photographs, a party and a small farewell gift could mark the occasion.

10. Write a closing record, together, if appropriate.

Finally, it might help readers to suggest that not all endings are like the closing of a door but rather like the closing of a book. Hopefully, you can close this one carrying with you some ideas for further study. It marks the beginning of learning which, in social work, never ends. Every situation and every client teaches us this.

References

Ahmad, A. (1990) *Practice with Care*, London, Race Equality Unit/ National Institute for Social Work.

Aros-Atolagbe, J. (1990) 'Soapbox', *Social Work Today*, vol. 21, no. 35, p. 36.

Atkinson, D. (1986) 'Engaging Competent Others: a Study of the Support Networks of People with Mental Handicap', *British Journal of Social Work*, vol. 16, Supplement, pp. 83–101.

Bacon, R. (1988) 'Counter-transference in a Case Conference: Resistance and Rejection in Work with Abusing Families and their Children', in Pearson, G., Treseder, J. and Yelloly, M. (eds) *Social Work and the Legacy of Freud: Psychoanalysis and its Uses,* Basingstoke, Macmillan Education.

Bailey, R. and Brake, M. (eds) (1975) *Radical Social Work*, London, Edward Arnold.

Ballard, R. and Rosser, P. (1979) 'Social Network Assembly', in Brandon, D. and Jordan, B. (eds) *Creative Social Work*, Oxford, Basil Blackwell.

Bandura, A. (1977) *Social Learning Theory*, Englewood Cliffs, N.J. Prentice-Hall.

Bar-On, A. A. (1990) 'Organisational Resource Mobilisation: a hidden face of social work practice', *British Journal of Social Work*, vol. 20, no. 2, pp. 133–49.

Bayley, M., Parker, P., Seyd, R. and Tennant, A. (1987) *Practising Community Care: developing locally-based practice*, University of Sheffield, Joint Unit for Social Services Research.

Beck, A. T. (1989) *Cognitive Therapy and the Emotional Disorders*, Harmondsworth, Penguin.

Benn, C. (1981) *Attacking Poverty through Participation: a community approach*, Sydney, Pit Publishing.

Bettelheim, B. (1988) *The Uses of Enchantment: the meaning and importance of Fairy Tales*, Harmondsworth, Penguin.

Bhaduri, R. (1990) 'Counselling with Karma', *Social Work Today*, vol. 21, no. 33, p. 16.

Black, D. (1979) 'Early Help for the Bereaved Child avoids later problems', *Modern Medicine*, 17 May, pp. 49–52.

178

Bowen, M. (1978) *Family Therapy in Clinical Practice*, New York, Jason Aronson.

Box, S., Copley, B., Magagna, J. and Moustaki, E. (eds), (1981) *Psychotherapy with Families: an Analytical Approach*, London, Routledge & Kegan Paul.

Boyce, L. and Anderson, S. (1990) 'A Common Bond', *Social Work Today*, vol. 21, no. 34, p. 38.

Brewster, B. (1988) *Supervision and Management in Social Work*, London, Central Council for Education and Training in Social Work.

Brown, A. (1986) *Groupwork*, London, Heinemann Educational Books.

Bryer, M. (1989) *Planning in Child Care: a Guide for Team Leaders and their teams*, London, British Agencies for Adoption and Fostering.

Buckle, J. (1981) *Intake Teams*, London, Tavistock Publications.

Burnham, J. B. (1986) *Family Therapy: First Steps Towards a Systemic Approach*, London, Tavistock Publications.

Butler, J., Bow, I. and Gibbons, J. (1978) 'Task-Centred Casework with Marital Problems', *British Journal of Social Work*, vol. 8, no. 4, pp.393–409.

Byng-Hall, J. and Campbell, D. (1981) 'Resolving Conflicts in Family Distance Regulation: an Integrative Approach', *Journal of Marital and Family Therapy*, vol. 7, no. 3, pp. 321–30.

Bywaters, P. (1975) 'Ending Casework Relationships', *Social Work Today*, vol. 6, no. 10, pp. 301–4 and vol. 6, no. 11, pp. 336–8.

Caplan, G. (1964) *Principles of Preventive Psychiatry*, London, Tavistock Publications.

Carpenter, J. and Treacher, A. (1989) *Problems and Solutions in Marital and Family Therapy*, Oxford, Basil Blackwell.

CCETSW/IAMHW (1989) *Multidisciplinary Teamwork: Models of Good Practice*, London, Central Council for Education and Training in Social Work.

Challis, D. and Chesterman, J. (1985) 'A System of Monitoring Social Work Activity with the Frail Elderly', *British Journal of Social Work*, vol. 15, no. 2, pp. 115–32.

Challis, D., Chessum, R., Chesterman, J., Luckett, R. and Traske, K. (1990) *Case Management in Social and Health Care*, Canterbury, Personal Social Services Research Unit.

Challis, D. and Davies, B. (1989) *Case Management in Community Care*, Aldershot, Gower.

Clulow, C. and Mattinson, J. (1989) *Marriage Inside Out*, Harmondsworth, Penguin.

Corby, B. (1982) 'Theory and Practice in Long-Term Social Work: a Case Study of Practice with Social Service Department Clients', *British Journal of Social Work*, vol. 12, no. 6, pp. 619–38.

Corey, G., Corey, M. S., Callanan, P. J. and Russell, J. M. (1982) *Group Techniques*, California, Brooks/Cole.

Corey, G. (1986) *Manual for Theory and Practice of Counselling and Psychotherapy* (Third edn), Monterey, Brooks/Cole.

180 References

Cornish, P. M. (1983) *Activities for the Frail-Aged*, Bicester, Winslow Press.

Corrigan, P. and Leonard, P. (1978) *Social Work Practice Under Capitalism: a Marxist Approach*, London, Macmillan.

Coulshed, V. (1990) *Management in Social Work*, Basingstoke, Macmillan Education.

Coulshed, V. and Abdullah-Zadeh, J. (1985) 'The Side Effects of Intervention', *British Journal of Social Work*, vol. 15, no. 5, pp. 479–86.

Dale, P., Davies, M., Morrison, T. and Waters, J. (1986) *Dangerous Families: Assessment and Treatment of Child Abuse*, London, Tavistock Publications.

Dana, M. and Lawrence, M. (1988) 'Understanding Bulimia: a Feminist, Psychoanalytic Account of Women's Eating Problems', in Pearson, G., Treseder, J. and Yelloly, M. (eds), *Social Work and the Legacy of Freud: Psychoanalysis and its Uses*, Basingstoke, Macmillan Education.

Davies, M. (1985) *The Essential Social Worker: a Guide to Positive Practice*, Aldershot, Wildwood House.

Davies, B. and Knapp, M. (eds) (1988) 'The Production of Welfare Approach: Evidence and Argument from the PSSRU', *British Journal of Social Work*, vol. 18, Supplement.

Department of Health (1988) *Protecting Children: a Guide for Social Workers Undertaking a Comprehensive Assessment*, London, HMSO.

Department of Health, Cmnd. 849 (1989) *Caring for People: Community Care in the Next Decade and Beyond*, London, HMSO.

Department of Health/SSI (1989a) *Homes are for Living In*, London, HMSO.

Department of Heath/Social Services Inspectorate (1990) *Caring for Quality: Guidance on Standards for Residential Homes for Elderly People*, London, HMSO.

Devore, W. and Schlesinger, E. C. (1981) *Ethnic-Sensitive Social Work Practice*, St Louis, C.V. Mosby Co.

Dickson, A. (1982) *A Woman in Your Own Right: Assertiveness and You*, London, Quartet.

Dillon, J. T. (1990) *The Practice of Questioning*, London, Routledge.

Dimmock, B. and Dungworth, D. (1985) 'Beyond the Family: Using Network Meetings with Statutory Child Care Cases', *Journal of Family Therapy*, vol. 7, no. 1, pp. 45–68.

Dominelli, L. (1988) *Anti-Racist Social Work*, Basingstoke, Macmillan Education.

Dominelli, L. and McLeod, E. (1989) *Feminist Social Work*, Basingstoke, Macmillan Education.

Downes, C. (1988) 'A Psychodynamic Approach to the Work of an Area Team', in Pearson, G., Treseder, J. and Yelloly, M. (eds), *Social Work and the Legacy of Freud: Psychoanalysis and its Uses*, Basingstoke, Macmillan Education.

Egan, G. (1981) *The Skilled Helper: a Model for Systematic Helping and Interpersonal Relating*, California, Brooks/Cole.

Ellis, A. (1962) *Reason and Emotion in Psychotherapy*, New York, Lyle Stuart.

England, H. (1986) *Social Work as Art: Making Sense for Good Practice*, London, Allen & Unwin.

Epstein, L. (1980) *Helping People: the Task-Centred Approach*, St Louis, C.V. Mosby.

Erikson, E. (1965) *Childhood and Society*, Harmondsworth, Penguin.

Fischer, J. (1976) *The Effectiveness of Social Casework*, New York, Charles C. Thomas.

Forder, A. (1974) *Concepts in Social Administration: a Framework for Analysis*, London Routledge & Kegan Paul.

Freed, A. O. (1988) 'Interviewing through an Interpreter', *Social Work*, vol. 33, no. 4, pp. 315–19.

Freire, P. (1972) *Pedagogy of the Oppressed*, Harmondsworth, Penguin.

Garrett, A. (1972) *Interviewing: its Principles and Methods*, New York, Family Service Association of America.

Garrison, J. E. and Howe, J. (1976) 'Community Intervention with the Elderly: a Social Network Approach', *Journal of the American Geriatric Society*, vol. 24, pp. 329–33.

Gibbons, J. S., Bow, I., Butler, J. and Powell, J. (1979) 'Clients' Reactions to Task-Centred Casework: a Follow-up Study', *British Journal of Social Work*, vol. 9, no. 2, pp. 203–15.

Golan, N. (1978) *Treatment in Crisis Situations*, New York, The Free Press.

Goldberg, E. M., Gibbons, J. and Sinclair, I. (1985) *Problems, Tasks and Outcomes: the Evaluation of Task-centred Casework in Three Settings*, London, George Allen & Unwin.

Goldberg, E. M., Walker, D. and Robinson, J. (1977) 'Exploring the Task-Centred Casework method', *Social Work Today*, vol. 9, no. 2, pp. 9–14.

Gorell Barnes, G. (1984) *Working with Families*, London, Macmillan Education.

Gottman, J., Notarius, C., Gonso, J. and Markman, H. (1977) *A Couple's Guide to Communication: Skills Teaching for Couples*, New York, Research Press.

Hadley, R., Cooper, M., Dale, P. and Stacy, G. (1987) *A Community Social Worker's Handbook*, London, Tavistock.

Haley, J. (1976) *Problem-Solving Therapy*, San Francisco, Jossey-Bass.

Hall, E. (1987) 'The Gender of the Therapist: its Relevance to Practice and Training', in Horobin, G. (ed.), *Sex, Gender and Care Work*, London, Jessica Kingsley.

Hanmer, J. and Statham, D. (1988) *Women and Social Work: Towards a Woman-Centred Practice*, Basingstoke, Macmillan Education.

Hardiker, P. and Barker, F. M. (eds) (1981) *Theories of Practice in Social Work*, London, Academic Press.

Hawkins, P. and Shohet, R. (1989) *Supervision in the Helping Profes-sions*, Milton Keynes, Open University Press.

Heap, K. (1985) *The Practice of Social Work with Groups: a Systematic Approach*, London, George Allen & Unwin.

Henderson, P. and Thomas, D. N. (1980) *Skills in Neighbourhood Work*, London, George Allen & Unwin.

Hirayama, H. and Cetingok, M. (1988) 'Empowerment: a Social Work Approach for Asian Immigrants', *Social Casework*, vol. 69, no. 1, pp. 41–7.

Hodgkinson, P. and Stewart, M. (1991) *Coping with Catastrophe: a professional handbook for post-disaster aftercare*, London, Routledge.

Hollis, F. (1964) *Casework: a Psychosocial Therapy*, New York, Random House.

Hollis, F. (1970) 'The Psychosocial Approach to the Practice of Case-work', in Roberts, R. W. and Nee, R. H. (eds), *Theories of Social Casework*, Chicago, University of Chicago Press.

Howe, D. (1987) *An Introduction to Social Work Theory: Making Sense in Practice*, Aldershot, Wildwood House.

Hudson, B. L. (1975) 'An Inadequate Personality', *Social Work Today*, vol. 6, no. 16, pp. 506–8.

Hudson, B. L. and Macdonald, G. M. (1986) *Behavioural Social Work: an Introduction*, London, Macmillan Education.

Jacobs, M. (1985) *Swift to Hear: Facilitating Skills in Listening and Responding*, London, SPCK.

Jacobs, M. (1986) *The Presenting Past: an Introduction to Practical, Psychodynamic Counselling*, London, Harper & Row.

James, A. L. and Wilson, K. (1986) *Couples, Conflict and Change*, London, Tavistock Publications.

Jervis, M. (1990) 'Family Fortunes', *Social Work Today*, vol. 21, no. 47, pp. 16–17.

Jones, C. (1983) *State Social Work and the Working Class*, London, Macmillan.

Jordan, B. (1972) *The Social Worker in Family Situations*, London, Routledge & Kegan Paul.

Jordan, B. (1987) 'Fallen Idol', *Community Care*, 12 February, pp. 24–5.

Kaufman, P. (1966) 'Helping People who Cannot Manage their Lives', *Children*, vol. 13, no. 3.

Kell, B. L. and Mueller, W. J. (1966) *Impact and Change: a Study of Counselling Relationships*, New York, Meredith Publishing Co.

Kelly, G. A. (1955) *The Psychology of Personal Constructs*, New York, Norton.

Langrish, S. V. (1981) 'Assertiveness Training', in Cooper, C. (ed.) *Improving Skills in Interpersonal Relations*, Aldershot, Gower.

Lau, A. (1984) 'Transcultural Issues in Family Therapy', *Journal of Family Therapy*, vol. 6, no. 2, pp. 91–112.

Lindemann, E. (1965) 'Symptomatology and Management of Acute Grief', in Parad, H. J. (ed.), *Crisis Intervention: Selected Readings*, New York, Family Service Association of America.

Liverpool, V. (1986) 'When Backgrounds Clash', *Community Care*, 2 October, pp. 19–21.

Lyons, J. (1977) *Chomsky*, London, Fontana/Collins.

Magee, B. (1982) *Men of Ideas*, Oxford, Oxford University Press.

Mahrer, A. R. (1989) *The Integration of Psychotherapies*, New York, Human Sciences Press.

Mainprice, J. (1974) *Marital Interaction and some Illnesses in Children*, Institute of Marital Studies, London, The Tavistock Institute of Human Relations.

Marris, P. (1986) *Loss and Change*, London, Routledge.

Marshall, M. (ed.) (1990) *Working with Dementia: Guidelines for Professionals*, Birmingham, Venture Press.

Marziali, E. (1988) 'The First Session: an Interpersonal Encounter', *Social Casework*, vol. 69, no. 1, pp. 23–7.

Mattinson, J. (1975) *The Reflection Process in Casework Supervision*, Institute of Marital Studies, London, The Tavistock Institute of Human Relations.

Mattinson, J. and Sinclair, I. (1979) *Mate and Stalemate: Working with Marital Problems in a Social Services Department*, Oxford, Basil Blackwell.

Maximé, J. E. (1986) 'Some Psychological Models of Black Self-Concept', in Ahmed, S., Cheetham, J. and Small, J. (eds) *Social Work with Black Children and their Families*, London, B. T. Batsford/British Agencies for Adoption and Fostering.

Mayer, J. E. and Timms, N. (1970) *The Client Speaks: Working-Class Impressions of Casework*, London, Routledge & Kegan Paul.

Meichenbaum, D. (1978) *Cognitive Behavior Modification: an Integrative Approach*, New York, Plenum Press.

Membership Notes (1990) British Assoc. of Counselling, Rugby.

Merry, T. (1990) 'Client-centred therapy: some trends and some troubles', *Counselling*, vol. 1, no. 1, pp. 17–18.

Minuchin, S. (1974) *Families and Family Therapy*, London, Tavistock Publications.

Mitchell, J. (1984) *Women: the Longest Revolution: Essays in Feminism, Literature and Psychoanalysis*, London, Virago.

Morgan, S. (1986) 'Practice in a Community Nursery for Black Children', in Ahmed, S., Cheetham, J. and Small, J. (eds) *Social Work with Black Children and their Families*, London, B. T. Batsford/British Agencies for Adoption and Fostering.

Moyes, B. (1988) 'The psychodynamic method in social work: some indications and contraindications', *Practice*, vol. 2, no. 3, pp. 236–42.

Neill, J. (1989) *Assessing Elderly People for Residential Care: a Practical Guide*, London, National Institute for Social Work.

Nelson-Jones, R. (1983) *Practical Counselling Skills*, New York, Holt, Rinehart & Winston.

Neville, D. and Beak, D. (1990) 'Solving the Case History Mystery', *Social Work Today*, vol. 21, no. 42, pp. 16–17.

Noonan, E. (1983) *Counselling Young People*, London, Methuen.

184   *References*

Northen, H. (1969) *Social Work with Groups*, New York, Columbia University Press.
Northen, H. (1982) *Clinical Social Work*, New York, Columbia University Press.
O'Brian, C. (1990) 'Family Therapy with Black Families', *Journal of Family Therapy*, vol. 12, no. 1, pp. 3–16.
O'Connor, G. G. (1988) 'Case Management: System and Practice', *Social Casework*, vol. 69, no. 2, pp. 97–106.
O'Hagan, K. (1986) *Crisis Intervention in Social Services*, London, Macmillan Education.
Orten, J. D. and Rich, L. L. (1988) 'A Model for Assessment of Incestuous Families', *Social Casework*, vol. 69, no. 10, pp. 611–19.
Papell, C. P. and Rothman, B. (1966) 'Social Groupwork Models: Possession and Heritage', *Journal of Education for Social Work*, vol. 2, no. 2, pp. 66–77.
Parad, H. J. and Caplan, G. (1965) 'A Framework for Studying Families in Crisis', in Parad, H. J. (ed.), *Crisis Intervention: Selected Readings*, New York, Family Service Association of America.
Parkes, C. M. (1986) *Bereavement: Studies of Grief in Adult Life*, London, Tavistock Publications.
Parry, G. (1990) *Coping with Crises*, Leicester, The British Psychological Society/Routledge.
Payne, M. (1986) *Social Care in the Community*, Basingstoke, Macmillan Education.
Pearson, G., Treseder, J. and Yelloly, M. (eds) (1988) *Social Work and the Legacy of Freud: Psychoanalysis and its Uses*, Basingstoke, Macmillan Education.
Penn, P. (1982) 'Circular Questioning', *Family Process*, vol. 21, no. 3, pp. 267–79.
Perelberg, R. J. and Miller, A. C. (eds) (1990) *Gender and Power in Families*, London, Tavistock/Routledge.
Perlman, H. H. (1957) *Social Casework: a Problem-Solving Process*, Chicago, University of Chicago Press.
Pilalis, J. (1986) 'The Integration of Theory and Practice: a re-examination of a paradoxical expectation', *British Journal of Social Work*, vol. 16, no. 1, pp. 79–96.
Pilalis, J. and Anderton, J. (1986) 'Feminism and Family Therapy: a possible meeting-point', *Journal of Family Therapy*, vol. 8, no. 2, pp. 99–114.
Preston-Shoot, M. (1987) *Effective Groupwork*, London, Macmillan Education.
Rack, P. (1982) *Race, Culture and Mental Disorder*, London, Tavistock Publications.
Randall, P. (1990) 'Too Old to Learn new Tricks?' *Community Care*, 1 March, pp. 20–21.
Raphael, B. (1984) *The Anatomy of Bereavement: a handbook for the caring professions*, London, Unwin Hyman.

Raphael, B. (1986) *When Disaster Strikes: a Handbook for the Caring Professions*, London, Hutchinson.

Rapoport, L. (1970) 'Crisis Intervention as a Brief Mode of Treatment', in Roberts, R. W. and Nee, R. H. (eds), *Theories of Social Casework*, Chicago, University of Chicago Press.

Redgrave, K. (1987) *Child's Play: 'Direct' Work with the Deprived Child,* Cheadle, Boys' and Girls' Welfare Society.

Redl, F. (1951) 'Art of Group Composition', in Schultze, S. (ed.), *Creative Living in a Children's Institution*, New York, Association Press.

Reed, B. G. and Garvin, C. D. (eds) (1983) *Groupwork with Women, Groupwork with Men: an Overview of Gender Issues in Social Group-work Practice*, New York, Haworth Press.

Reid, W. J. (1978) *The Task-Centred System*, New York, Columbia University Press.

Reid, W. J. and Epstein, L. (1972) *Task-Centred Casework*, New York, Columbia University Press.

Reid, W. J. and Epstein, L. (eds) (1977) *Task-Centred Practice*, New York, Columbia University Press.

Reid, W. J. and Hanrahan, P. (1981) 'The Effectiveness of Social Work: Recent Evidence', in Goldberg, E. M. and Connolly, N. (eds), *Evaluative Research in Social Care*, London, Heinemann.

Reid, W. J. and Shyne, A. W. (1969) *Brief and Extended Casework*, New York, Columbia University Press.

Rich, J. (1968) *Interviewing Children and Adolescents*, London, Macmillan.

Richmond, M. (1922) *What is Social Case Work?*, New York, Russell Sage.

Rogers, C. (1980) *A Way of Being*, Boston, Mass., Houghton Mifflin.

Rojek, C. (1986) 'The 'Subject' in Social Work', *British Journal of Social Work*, vol. 16, no. 1, pp. 65–77.

Rojek, C., Peacock, G. and Collins, S. (1988) *Social Work and Received Ideas*, London, Routledge.

Rueveni, U. (1979) *Networking Families in Crisis*, New York, Human Sciences Press.

Runciman, P. (1989) 'Health Assessment of the Elderly: a multidisciplin-ary perspective', in Taylor, R. and Ford, J. (eds), *Social Work and Health Care*, London, Jessica Kingsley.

Sainsbury, E. (1986) 'The Contribution of Client Studies to Social Work Practice', in Wedge, P. (ed.), *Social Work – Research into Practice*, Birmingham, British Association of Social Workers.

Schless, A. P., Teichman, A., Mendels, J. and Di Giacomo, J. N. (1977) 'The Role of Stress as a Precipitating Factor of Psychiatric Illness', *British Journal of Psychiatry*, vol. 130, pp. 19–22.

Schutz, W. C. (1966) *FIRO: the Interpersonal Underworld*, New York, Science and Behavior Books.

Scott, M. (1983) *Group Parent-Training Programme*, Liverpool Personal

Service Society, Stanley Street, Liverpool, L1 6AN.

Scott, M. (1989) *A Cognitive Behavioural Approach to Clients' Problems*, London, Routledge.

Scott, M. J. and Stradling, S. G. (1990) 'Group Cognitive Therapy for Depression Produces Clinically Significant Reliable Change in Community-Based Settings', *Behavioural Psychotherapy*, vol. 18, pp. 1–19.

Scrutton, S. (1989) *Counselling Older People: a Creative Response to Ageing*, London, Edward Arnold.

Sharkey, P. (1989) 'Social Networks and Social Service Workers', *British Journal of Social Work*, vol. 19, no. 5, pp. 387–405.

Sheik, S. (1986) 'An Asian Mothers' Self-Help Group', in Ahmed, S., Cheetham, J. and Small, J. (eds), *Social Work with Black Children and their Families*, London, B. T. Batsford/British Agencies for Adoption and Fostering.

Sheldon, B. (1983) 'The Use of Single-Case Experimental Designs in the Evaluation of Social Work', *British Journal of Social Work*, vol. 13, no. 5, pp. 477–500.

Sheldon, B. (1984) 'Behavioural Approaches with Psychiatric Patients', in Olsen, M. R. (ed.), *Social Work and Mental Health*, London Tavistock Publications.

Shulman, L. (1979) *The Skills of Helping: Individuals and Groups*, Itasca, Illinois, Peacock.

Simmonds, J. (1988) 'Thinking about Feelings in Group Care', in Pearson, G., Treseder, J. and Yelloly, M. (eds), *Social Work and the Legacy of Freud: Psychoanalysis and its Uses*, London, Macmillan Education.

Social Information Systems (1990) *Social Services and Quality Assurance*, Manchester, SIS Ltd.

Solomon, B. B. (1976) *Black Empowerment: Social Work with Oppressed Communities*, New York, Columbia University Press.

Speck, R. V. (1967) 'Psychotherapy of the Social Network of a Schizophrenic Family, *Family Process*, vol. 7, pp. 208–14.

Spurling, L. (1988) 'Casework as Dialogue: a Story of Incest', in Pearson, G., Treseder, J. and Yelloly, M. (eds), *Social Work and the Legacy of Freud: Psychoanalysis and its Uses*, Basingstoke, Macmillan Education.

Stevenson, O. (1963) 'The Understanding Caseworker', *New Society*, 1 August, pp. 84–96.

Stewart, I. (1989) *Transactional Analysis Counselling in Action*, London, Sage Publications.

Thoburn, J. (1988) *Child Placement: Principles and Practice*, Aldershot, Wildwood House.

Treacher, A. and Carpenter, J. (eds) (1984) *Using Family Therapy*, Oxford, Basil Blackwell.

Truax, C. B. and Carkhuff, R. R. (1967) *Towards Effective Counselling and Psychotherapy*, Chicago, Aldine.

Tsoi, M. and Yule, J. (1982) 'Building up New Behaviours: Shaping, Prompting and Fading', in Yule, W. and Carr, J. (eds), *Behaviour Modification for the Mentally Handicapped*, London, Croom Helm.

Tuckman, B. W. and Jensen, M. A. C. (1977) 'Stages of Small Group Development Revisited', *Group and Organisation Studies*, vol. 2, no. 4, pp. 419–27.

Tully, J. B. (1976) 'Personal Construct Theory and Psychological Changes Related to Social Work Training', *British Journal of Social Work*, vol. 6, no. 4, pp. 481–99.

Twelvetrees, A. (1991) *Community Work*, 2nd edn, London, Macmillan Education.

Van der Velden, H. E. M., Halevy-Martinin, J., Ruhf, L. and Schoen-field, P. (1984) 'Conceptual Issues in Network Therapy', *International Journal of Family Therapy*, vol. 6, no. 2, pp. 68–81.

Vernon, S., Harris, R. and Ball, C. (1990) *Towards Social Work Law: Legally Competent Professional Practice,* Paper 4.2. London, CCETSW.

Vickery, A. (1976) 'A Unitary Approach to Social Work with the Mentally Disordered', in Olsen, M. R. (ed.), *Differential Approaches in Social Work with the Mentally Disordered*, Birmingham, British Association of Social Workers.

Walker, L. (1978) 'Work with a Parents' Group', in McCaughan, N. (ed.) *Group Work: Learning and Practice*, London, George Allen & Unwin.

Walrond-Skinner, S. (ed.) (1979) *Family and Marital Psychotherapy: a Critical Approach*, London, Routledge & Kegan Paul.

Webb, S. A. and McBeath, G. B. (1990) 'Political Critique of Kantian Ethics: a Reply to Professor R. S. Downie', *British Journal of Social Work*, vol. 20, no. 1, pp. 65–71.

Whan, M. (1983) 'Tricks of the Trade: Questionable Theory and Practice in Family Therapy', *British Journal of Social Work*, vol. 13, no. 3, pp. 321–38.

Whitaker, D. S. (1975) 'Some Conditions for Effective Work with Groups', *British Journal of Social Work*, vol. 5, no. 4, pp. 423–40.

Whitaker, D. S. (1985) *Using Groups to Help People*, London, Routledge & Kegan Paul.

Winnicott, D. W. (1957) 'The Capacity to Be Alone', paper read at a meeting of the British Psychoanalytical Society, 24 July.

Wittenberg, I. S. (1970) *Psychoanalytic Insight and Relationships; a Kleinian Approach*, London, Routledge & Kegan Paul.

Wootten, B. F. (1959) *Social Science and Social Pathology*, London, George Allen & Unwin.

Yalom, I. D. (1970) *The Theory and Practice of Group Psychotherapy*, New York, Basic Books.

Yelloly, M. A. (1980) *Social Work Theory and Psychoanalysis*, Woking-ham, Van Nostrand Reinhold.

Zastrow, C. (1985) *Social Work with Groups*, Chicago, Nelson-Hall.

Index